1 CORINTHIANS

J. Vernon McGee

THOMAS NELSON PUBLISHERS

Nashville • Atlanta • London • Vancouver

Copyright © 1991 by Thru the Bible Radio

Published in Nashville, Tennessee, by Thomas Nelson, Inc.

Scripture quotations are from the KING JAMES VERSION of the Bible.

Library of Congress Cataloging-in-Publication Data

McGee, J. Vernon (John Vernon), 1904–1988
   [Thru the Bible with J. Vernon McGee]
   Thru the Bible commentary series / J. Vernon McGee.
     p.   cm.
   Reprint. Originally published: Thru the Bible with J. Vernon McGee. 1975.
   Includes bibliographical references.
   ISBN 0-7852-1048-2 (TR)
   ISBN 0-7852-1107-1 (NRM)
   1. Bible—Commentaries. I. Title.
BS491.2.M37 1991
220.7′7—dc20   90-41340
                                      CIP

Printed in the United States of America
3 4 5 6 7 8 9 — 99 98 97 96

CONTENTS

1 CORINTHIANS

PREFACE

The radio broadcasts of the Thru the Bible Radio five-year program were transcribed, edited, and published first in single-volume paperbacks to accommodate the radio audience.

There has been a minimal amount of further editing for this publication. Therefore, these messages are not the word-for-word recording of the taped messages which went out over the air. The changes were necessary to accommodate a reading audience rather than a listening audience.

These are popular messages, prepared originally for a radio audience. They should not be considered a commentary on the entire Bible in any sense of that term. These messages are devoid of any attempt to present a theological or technical commentary on the Bible. Behind these messages is a great deal of research and study in order to interpret the Bible from a popular rather than from a scholarly (and too-often boring) viewpoint.

We have definitely and deliberately attempted "to put the cookies on the bottom shelf so that the kiddies could get them."

The fact that these messages have been translated into many languages for radio broadcasting and have been received with enthusiasm reveals the need for a simple teaching of the whole Bible for the masses of the world.

I am indebted to many people and to many sources for bringing this volume into existence. I should express my especial thanks to my secretary, Gertrude Cutler, who supervised the editorial work; to Dr. Elliott R. Cole, my associate, who handled all the detailed work with the publishers; and finally, to my wife Ruth for tenaciously encouraging me from the beginning to put my notes and messages into printed form.

Solomon wrote, ". . . of making many books there is no end; and much study is a weariness of the flesh" (Eccl. 12:12). On a sea of books that flood the marketplace, we launch this series of THRU THE BIBLE with the hope that it might draw many to the one Book, *The Bible.*

J. VERNON McGEE

The First Epistle
to the
CORINTHIANS

INTRODUCTION

Paul addressed this epistle to the church which was in the city of Corinth. He wrote it from Ephesus around A.D. 55–57 (more likely 57). Carnal Corinth was the sin center of the Roman Empire in Paul's day. It was labeled "Vanity Fair." Its location was about forty miles west of Athens on a narrow isthmus between Peloponnesus and the mainland. It was the great commercial center of the Roman Empire with three harbors, of which two were important: Lechaeum, about one and one half miles to the west, and Cenchrea, about eight and one half miles to the east. Since the time of Paul, a canal has been put through the isthmus, and Corinth is no longer an important city.

Even the ruins of Corinth were lost to history for many years. A fishing village had been built over them. In 1928 an earthquake uncovered them, and now much of the city has been excavated.

During that time in history when Greece was independent, Corinth was the head of the Achaean League. Later, in 196 B.C., Rome declared it a free city. In 146 B.C. Corinth rebelled and was totally destroyed by Mummius, the Roman general. Its art treasures were taken to Rome and for a century it lay desolate. One hundred years later, in 46 B.C., Julius Caesar rebuilt the city in great elegance, restoring it to its former prominence and returning its former splendor.

In Paul's day there were about four hundred thousand inhabitants in Corinth. It was located on this important isthmus, as we previously mentioned, and the commerce of the world flowed through the two harbors connected with the city of Corinth. The population consisted of Greeks, Jews, Italians, and a mixed multitude. Sailors, merchants, adventurers, and refugees from all corners of the Roman Empire filled its streets. A perpetual "Vanity Fair" was held here. The vices of the East and of the West met and clasped hands in the work of human degradation.

Religion itself was put to ignoble uses. A magnificent temple was built for the Greek goddess Aphrodite, or Venus as we know her by the Roman name. In it were a thousand priestesses who ministered to a base worship. Those thousand so-called priestesses were actually nothing in the world but prostitutes. Sex was a religion there. I believe that Corinth could teach this generation about sex. However, I think this generation already knows enough about that subject. We are overwhelmed with it *ad nauseam* today.

Not only was their religion debased, but the Greek philosophy was in its decay also. The city was given over to licentiousness and pleasure. The Isthmian games were conducted here. The people went on in endless discussions. It was into this kind of setting that Paul came, and later he said, "For I determined not to know any thing among you, save Jesus Christ, and him crucified" (1 Cor. 2:2). This was a people given over to pleasure, debauchery, and drunkenness. In fact, they coined a word in the Roman Empire which was to "corinthianize." Believe me, when you would "corinthianize," it meant that you went to the very limit in sin.

Against this corrupt background Paul preached the gospel in Corinth. He founded a church there and later wrote two epistles to them. Paul came to Corinth on his second missionary journey, and it was the terminus of his third missionary journey. Acts 18:1–18 gives us the account of eighteen months spent in Corinth. It was in Corinth that he met Aquila and Priscilla. They had been driven out of Rome by an edict of Emperor Claudius. Suetonius writes that this edict was issued because of tumults raised by the Jews who were persecuting their Christian brethren.

When Paul first came to Corinth, he preached in the synagogue. As usual, a riot was the result. Paul usually had a riot, revolution, and revival wherever he went. Corinth was no exception.

On Paul's third journey he spent a long period of time in Ephesus. It was in Ephesus that he did some of his outstanding work as a missionary. Probably that area was more thoroughly evangelized than any other. However, this caused the Corinthians to become disturbed. They were baby Christians, and they were urging Paul to come to them. Apparently Paul wrote them a letter to correct some of the errors that had come into that church. They, in turn, wrote to Paul asking questions that they wanted answered about political issues, religion, domestic problems, heathenism, and morality. Paul answered them and responded to more reports which were brought to him. We do not have that first letter which Paul wrote to them. The letter that followed the reports brought to him is the letter we know today as 1 Corinthians. That is the epistle we are about to study. Later on Paul wrote the letter we now call 2 Corinthians.

The keynote of this epistle is the supremacy of Christ, the Lordship of Jesus. That is so important for us to note because that is the solution to the problems. You will find here that He is the solution to correct moral, social, and ecclesiastical disorders.

In this epistle we will also find the true doctrine of the Resurrection set forth. That makes this epistle tremendously significant.

A broad outline of this book divides it into three major divisions:
1. Salutation and thanksgiving, 1:1–9
2. Carnalities, 1:10—11:34
   (Conditions in the Corinthian church)
3. Spiritualities, 12—16
   (Spiritual gifts)

The spiritualities are far more important than the carnalities. I think we need to realize that over nineteen hundred years ago the church in Corinth was beset with problems. They had lost sight of the main objective, and they had gotten away from the person of Christ. As a consequence, they were overwhelmed with these problems.

Our contemporary church is likewise beset with problems. It is almost shocking to discover that the problems of the church today are the same as they were in Corinth over nineteen hundred years ago. I believe that the real problem today is that we have lost sight of the centrality of Christ crucified. We have lost sight of the Lordship of Jesus Christ. That was the problem then, and it is still the problem now. Our study of this epistle should be a relevant and pertinent study for us.

OUTLINE

CHAPTER 1

THEME: Centrality of Christ crucified; correction of divisions

SALUTATION AND THANKSGIVING

Paul, called to be an apostle of Jesus Christ through the will of God, and Sosthenes our brother [1 Cor. 1:1].

Will you notice in your Bible that the little verb "to be" is in italics, which means it is not in the original. It should read, "Paul, called an apostle." This declares what kind of an apostle he is. He is a called apostle. God called him; the Lord Jesus Christ waylaid him on the Damascus road. Then the Spirit of God taught him yonder in the desert of Arabia. He is a *called* apostle.

He is an apostle of Jesus Christ "through the will of God." It is the will of God that made him an apostle. This is so important.

It is wonderful today to be able to say, "I am where I am and I am doing what I am doing because of the will of God." Is that your situation? If you can say that, then I do not need to add that you are a very happy, joyful Christian. You are not only a happy, joyful Christian, but you are one who is well-oriented into life. You have no frustrations. Of course you may have disturbing experiences occasionally, but deep down underneath there is that tremendous satisfaction. Paul had that when he could say that he was an apostle of Jesus Christ through the will of God.

"Sosthenes our brother"—apparently Sosthenes had brought the message from the church at Corinth, and now he is going to carry this epistle back to them. He is the one who is joining Paul in these greetings.

Unto the church of God which is at Corinth, to them that are sanctified in Christ Jesus, called to be saints, with all that in every place call upon the name of Jesus Christ our Lord, both theirs and ours [1 Cor. 1:2].

Notice it is "unto the church of God which is at Corinth." It is called the church of God because He is the One who is the Architect of the church. The letter is directed to the "sanctified in Christ Jesus."

The church is *at* Corinth, but it is *in* Christ Jesus. The address of the church is not important, but the person of Christ is all-important. What does it mean to be a Christian? It means to be in Christ! Whether you are at Corinth or at Los Angeles, at Ephesus or at New York City is incidental. The important question is: Are you in Christ Jesus?

Paul calls them "sanctified in Christ Jesus." The term *sanctification* is used in several different ways, as we have already seen in Romans. Here it is *positional* sanctification, which is the position we have in Christ. When sanctification is joined to God the Father or God the Son, the Lord Jesus Christ, then it is generally positional. When sanctification is connected with the Holy Spirit, then that is practical sanctification. We will learn in verse 30 that Christ has been made unto us sanctification—along with wisdom and righteousness and redemption. He is our sanctification.

You see, friend, you are not going to heaven until you are perfect— I am not either. And I am not perfect, not even near it. The fact of the matter is that if you knew me like I know myself, you wouldn't listen to me. But wait a minute! Don't tune me out because, if I knew you like you know yourself, I wouldn't speak to you. So let's just stay connected here, if you don't mind.

Sanctification is a position we have in Christ. If you have trusted Him, He has been made over to you your sanctification. You are as saved right now as you will be a million years from now because you are saved in Christ. You cannot add anything to that.

There is also a *practical* sanctification, which is something that varies. These Corinthians don't sound like sanctified saints. The work of the Holy Spirit was not very much in evidence in their lives. But they were *positionally* sanctified in Christ Jesus.

They were "called to be saints"—again, note that "to be" is in italics, which means it is not in the original. Just as Paul was a *called* apostle, they were *called* saints. We are also called saints. We do not become saints by what we do; we become saints because of our posi-

tion in Christ. The word *saint* actually means "set aside to God."
Every Christian should be set aside to God. For example, the pans and
vessels that were used in the tabernacle and later in the temple were
called holy vessels. Holy? Yes, because they were for the use of God.
On what basis is a child of God a saint or holy? On the basis that he is
for the use of God. This is the position that we have. I repeat again,
one is not a saint on the basis of what one does. All of mankind is
divided between the "saints" and the "ain'ts." If you "ain't" in Christ,
then you are an "ain't." If you are in Christ, then you are a "saint."

The Corinthians are called saints together "with all that in every
place call upon the name of Jesus Christ our Lord, both theirs and
ours." Possibly it would be more correct to say, "with all that in every
place, both theirs and ours, who call upon the name of Jesus Christ
our Lord." This also indicates that the teaching of this epistle is addressed to the church at large, which is composed of all who call
upon the Lord Jesus, whether it be in Corinth or elsewhere.

Now Paul uses his usual introduction: "grace and peace."

**Grace be unto you, and peace, from God our Father, and
from the Lord Jesus Christ [1 Cor. 1:3].**

Grace and *peace* are always in that sequence. Grace *(charis)* was the
word of greeting in the Greek world. Peace is the Hebrew *shalom,* a
form of greeting in the religious world. Paul combined these two
words and lifted them to the highest level. You and I are saved by the
grace of God; it is love in action. When we have been saved by the
grace of God, then we can have the peace of God in our hearts. Have
you received Christ as your Savior? Are your sins on Christ? If they
are, you will have peace in your heart because He bore your sins.
"Therefore being justified by faith, we have peace with God through
our Lord Jesus Christ" (Rom. 5:1). *Grace* and *peace* are two great
words.

**I thank my God always on your behalf, for the grace of
God which is given you by Jesus Christ [1 Cor. 1:4].**

"By Jesus Christ" would be better translated "in Jesus Christ" because it is in Christ that we have all of these blessings. We are blessed with all spiritual blessings in heavenly places in Christ (see Eph. 1:3). This is the place of blessing.

"Jesus Christ" should be Christ Jesus—*Christ* is His title, while *Jesus* is His human name. *Christ* is literally *anointed*, which is the official appellation of the long-promised Savior. Is it important to say Christ Jesus instead of Jesus Christ? It was to Paul. Paul tells us that he never knew Him after the flesh. That is, he didn't know the Jesus who walked this earth in the days of His flesh. He may have seen Him; I think he was present at the Crucifixion. But his first personal contact was with the resurrected Christ, and to Paul He was always the Lord of glory. In most of Paul's epistles it should read Christ Jesus rather than Jesus Christ.

That in every thing ye are enriched by him, in all utterance, and in all knowledge [1 Cor. 1:5].

This is what Paul is talking about in Colossians 3:16 when he says: "Let the word of Christ dwell in you richly in all wisdom; teaching and admonishing one another in psalms and hymns and spiritual songs, singing with grace in your hearts to the Lord." Since I can't sing it, I can say it; that is, I can talk about the Word of God. In some churches the Psalms are sung. I think the whole Bible could be put to music. But I couldn't sing it. The important thing is to have the Word of Christ in our hearts. That does not necessarily mean to memorize it. It means to obey it. If Christ is in your heart, you are obeying Him, and you are thinking upon Him. He occupies your mind and your heart. Some of the meanest little brats that I have ever met have memorized over a hundred verses of Scripture. That doesn't mean no one should memorize Scripture just because some mean brats have memorized it. It does mean that simply memorizing Scripture is not what is meant by hiding it in your heart. You hide it in your heart, my friend, when you obey Him, think about Him, are enriched in [not by] him." When He becomes the Lord in your life, it will solve many of your problems. That is what Paul is going to talk about in this epistle.

Even as the testimony of Christ was confirmed in you:

So that ye come behind in no gift; waiting for the coming of our Lord Jesus Christ [1 Cor. 1:6–7].

Here he intimates one of the problems that this church was having. They were carnal. They were occupied with only one gift. Paul says at the very beginning that he doesn't want them to come behind in any gift. There are many gifts. Paul wants all these gifts to be manifested in the church.

"Waiting for the coming of our Lord Jesus Christ" means that they are to be occupied with Him.

Who shall also confirm you unto the end, that ye may be blameless in the day of our Lord Jesus Christ [1 Cor. 1:8].

He says "blameless"; he does not say they will be faultless. There will always be someone who will find fault with you. But you are not to be worthy of blame. "That ye may be blameless in the day of our Lord Jesus Christ." And the "day of our Lord Jesus Christ" is not only referring to the present day, but to the day He will come and take His church out of the world. Paul will talk about that in this epistle also.

Now we come to the last verse of Paul's introduction, the salutation and thanksgiving. This verse could easily be passed over with the feeling that you hadn't missed very much. Yet I feel that verse 9 is probably the key to the epistle. It emphasizes that the Lord Jesus Christ is the solution to the problems that they had in the church and also to the personal problems that were present among the believers in Corinth. It is startling to note the similarities between the problems in the Corinthian church and the problems today. The solution is the same now as it was then.

God is faithful, by whom ye were called unto the fellowship of his Son Jesus Christ our Lord [1 Cor. 1:9].

Have you noticed that the Lord Jesus Christ is mentioned in this section in practically every verse? Actually, it isn't practically every verse; it is *every* verse. This is the ninth reference to Him in nine verses. It is obvious that Paul is putting an emphasis upon the person of the Lord Jesus Christ.

There is an extended name given to our Lord here—"called unto the fellowship of his Son Jesus Christ our Lord." This gives four points of identification for Him. So there is no way of misunderstanding.

He makes two tremendous statements: God is faithful, and we are called unto the fellowship of His Son.

"God is faithful." Men are not always faithful. Even believers are not always faithful. But God is faithful.

"By whom ye were called" is the high calling of God in Christ Jesus.

We are called "unto the fellowship of his Son Jesus Christ our Lord." The word that is important here in connection with the Lord Jesus Christ is *fellowship*. The word is the Greek *koinonia*, and it is used by Paul again and again. Actually, the word can have several different meanings. It can mean fellowship as we understand it today. It can be used to mean a contribution. In Romans 15:26 he says they made a certain *koinonia* for the poor saints which were at Jerusalem, and there it means a contribution. In 1 Corinthians 10:16 the word *koinonia* is used in connection with Communion. He is speaking of the Lord's Supper and writes: "The cup of blessing which we bless, is it not the [*koinonia*] communion of the blood of Christ? The bread which we break, is it not the [*koinonia*] communion of the body of Christ?"

Koinonia can also mean a partnership, and I believe that is the way it is used here in this ninth verse. "God is faithful, by whom ye were called unto the [partnership] fellowship of his Son Jesus Christ our Lord." Now this is without doubt one of the greatest privileges that is given to us. If you are in Christ, if you have come to Him and accepted Him as your Savior, then you are in partnership with Christ. He is willing to be our partner. Therefore this means an intimate relationship to Christ.

There are different kinds of partnerships. There can be a partnership in business. I know two men who are in partnership. These fellows were friends in the military service, and when they came out of the service years ago, they formed a partnership in business. One of them was converted to Christ; the other was not. It has been an unhappy partnership ever since then. They have a big business with a lot of investments and the partnership cannot be broken. It is a partnership, but it is not a happy one.

Then there is marriage with a partnership in a love relationship. This should be a very close, intimate relationship. There is a passage in the Old Testament that makes me smile because I know God had man and wife in mind when He wrote it. He said among other things that they were not to hitch an ox and an ass together for plowing. They were not to plow together. Well, in marriage I have seen many an ox and an ass hitched up together! That ought not to be because marriage is a partnership.

What does it mean, then, to be in partnership with the Lord Jesus? For one thing, it means that in business you own things together with Him. Everything that I own belongs to Jesus Christ. It belongs to Him as much as it does to me. Therefore, He is interested in what I own. Now I must confess that there was a time when I owned a few things that I don't think He cared about. There was a time when I very selfishly thought only of myself in connection with what I owned. But now, although I don't own too much—when He is in partnership with me, He is not in what you would call big business—what I have is His. I have a nice Chevrolet car because a wonderful dealer helped me get it. When I drove out with it, it was mine, but I told the Lord Jesus that it was His too. He has taken many a ride in it with me, by the way. Whatever I have is His also. I thank Him for my house, and I thank Him for taking care of it because it is His, too, you see. Whatever I have is His.

The marriage partnership means different things. It means having mutual interests. I'm in that kind of partnership with the Lord Jesus too. That means that Christ is interested in me and I am interested in Him. That carries it to a pretty high plane, you see. Also, we have a mutual devotion. His resources are mine, and mine are His. He doesn't get very much, but He owns me. I have presented my body to

Him. Now that answers quite a few questions for me about where I can go and what I can do. For example, I used to smoke quite a bit. Now I have metastatic cancer in the lungs, and it would be pretty foolish for me to smoke now. However, long ago when I made the discovery, not just that my body is the temple of the Holy Spirit, but also that Christ belongs to me and I belong to Christ, I wanted to give Him the best body that I could. That is when I gave up smoking. That decided the question for me. Do you see that our decisions are made on a higher plane than simply "Dare I do this?" or "Ought I do that?" We belong to Jesus Christ and Jesus Christ belongs to us.

Also in the love partnership there is a mutual service. God accommodates Himself to our weakness. I need His gentleness, and I accept His power. A verse of Scripture which deals with this is a verse that I believe has been mistranslated. This was called to my attention by G. Campbell Morgan. The verse is Isaiah 63:9: "In all their affliction he was afflicted, and the angel of his presence saved them: in his love and in his pity he redeemed them; and he bare them, and carried them all the days of old." It sounds as if in our weakness He becomes weak. The better translation puts it in the negative: "In all affliction he was *not* afflicted." That is a lot more meaningful to me. It means that when I stumble and fall, He does not stumble and fall. He accommodates Himself to my stumbling, my blindness, my ignorance, my weakness. Although He accommodates Himself to that, He does not become weak at all. I heard a preacher make the statement that if you get into trouble ignorantly without realizing it, or you are caught by circumstances, He will help you out of it. But if you go into sin deliberately and foolishly, He will let you alone rather than help you work it out. I am here to say that this has *not* been my experience. I have made many blunders, and I have stumbled, and I have fallen. Many times I have done it deliberately. Yet my Lord never let me down. He was always there. He accommodated Himself to my weakness. How wonderful that is, friend! The partnership of Jesus Christ is the solution to the problems of life.

Verse 9 concludes Paul's salutation. Actually, all the rest of the epistle is a big parenthesis until we come to 1 Corinthians 15:58: "Therefore, my beloved brethren, be ye stedfast, unmoveable, always abounding in the work of the Lord, forasmuch as ye know that your labour is not in vain in the Lord." "Therefore" gathers up all this marvelous epistle and goes way back here to verse 9. I can depend on the faithfulness of God "by whom ye were called unto the fellowship of his Son Jesus Christ our Lord."

It has taken me a long time to learn this. In fact, I have had to retire to learn this. I am just going ahead with Him as my partner. I face all of today's problems with Him as my partner. I can count on Him. I can look to Him. He is part and parcel of all of it. This is the solution to the problems and the frustrations of life, my beloved.

This concludes the introduction, which is a salutation and thanksgiving. The body of the epistle concerns conditions in the Corinthian church, and there were real problems, as we shall see.

DIVISIONS AND PARTY SPIRIT

Verse 10 begins a new section in Paul's first epistle to the Corinthian believers. He is addressing himself now to the primary problem in the Corinthian church. It is surprising to see that their problems have a very familiar ring. I don't know of a church today that does not have problems, and many of them are the same as those that the Corinthian believers faced.

CENTRALITY OF CHRIST CRUCIFIED
CORRECTS DIVISIONS

Now I beseech you, brethren, by the name of our Lord Jesus Christ, that ye all speak the same thing, and that there be no divisions among you; but that ye be perfectly joined together in the same mind and in the same judgment [1 Cor. 1:10].

Notice that the Lord Jesus Christ is again mentioned in this verse. This epistle emphasizes the lordship of Christ. We hear a great deal about His lordship, but we see very little of it today. For this reason the church and individual Christians have serious problems. It is not enough to talk about the lordship of Christ. Is He your Lord? Have you made Him your Lord and your Master?

"That ye all speak the same thing" doesn't mean that everyone must say the identical words. It means believers shouldn't be clawing one another to death, fighting with each other, hating each other.

The word for "divisions" is *schisma*. It means there should be no open break, no fracturing of the church, which is done by fighting, by gossip, criticism, hatred, or bitterness. Believe me, friend, I see that in many contemporary churches. These things cannot be in your life if Jesus Christ is your partner.

Let "there be no divisions among you; but that ye be perfectly joined together in the same mind and in the same judgment." What is "the same mind"? Well, it is the mind of Christ (see Phil. 2:5–8).

For it hath been declared unto me of you, my brethren, by them which are of the house of Chloe, that there are contentions among you [1 Cor. 1:11].

The word for "contentions" here is *eris*. Now Eris was the goddess of strife and wrangling. There was strife, quarreling, schisms, and wranglings in the church at Corinth. Paul got his information firsthand— he named his source—he said he got his information from Chloe. My friend, if you are going to make a charge, back it up with your name like Chloe did. When I first became pastor in downtown Los Angeles, a man came to me and said, "I want to tell you about a certain situation." He told me about a certain man and, believe me, it wasn't very nice. He wanted me to do something about it. He said, "You ought to bring this up before the board, and if they can't handle it, then it should be brought before the church." I answered, "Fine, that is the way it should be done. What night can you come?" "Oh!" he said, "I don't intend to come. You're the pastor, you are the one to handle it." I answered, "You are right. I am the one to handle it. I am the pastor now. However, you will need to be present to make the charge." "Oh," he said, "I won't do that." So I told him, "If you are not willing to sign your name to the charge, we will forget it." And we forgot it because he refused to back up the charge with his name. One must admire

Chloe there in Corinth. Chloe told it as it was, brought it out into the open, and said, "There is trouble in our church, bad trouble, and it needs to be dealt with."

My friend, when there is sin in the church, it is like a cancer. It needs to be dealt with. When I had cancer, I went to my doctor for help. Imagine him saying, "Now we don't want to get excited; we don't want to get disturbed; we don't want to become emotional; we don't want to cause any trouble. We want you to have a nice, peaceful mind; so I will sprinkle a little talcum powder on this place and everything will be all right." Well, friend, I would have smelled good, but I would have died of the cancer. You've got to deal with a cancer, and you've got to deal with trouble in the church. Woe to the man who exposes it, but if that is not done, the church is going to suffer. Of course it will!

The trouble with the church in Corinth was that they had a bunch of baby Christians. Babies generally do a lot of howling, you know. When I was a pastor in Pasadena, we had a nursery room for babies, and we called it The Bawl Room. I have learned that in some churches the entire church is a bawl room because of the bawling baby Christians.

Now this I say, that every one of you saith, I am of Paul; and I of Apollos; and I of Cephas; and I of Christ [1 Cor. 1:12].

Divisions were being caused by believers following different leaders of the church. They formed cliques around certain men. In one group were the proud pupils of Paul; in another the adoring admirers of Apollos, and there were some who liked Simon Peter, or Cephas, and they formed the chummy cult of Cephas.

We know quite a lot about Paul. He was intellectual, he was brilliant, and he was courageous—but apparently not attractive physically. Simon Peter was fiery. He had been weak at first, but he became a rugged preacher of the gospel. He had a great heart and was very emotional. Apollos was one of the great preachers of the apostolic church. He was not an apostle and has not been given much recognition, but he was a great preacher. I think he was the Billy Graham of that day. All three of these men had strong personalities, but they did not cause the divisions. They all contended together for the faith. They maintained the unity of the Spirit, and they all exalted Jesus Christ. It was the members of the church in Corinth who were guilty of making the divisions.

One little group said, "Oh, we love brother Paul because he's so spiritual." Another group said, "We like Simon Peter because he pounds the pulpit and is so evangelistic." Another said, "We love this man Apollos. He soars to the heights, and he reaches the multitudes." They were not taking into account the fact that all three of them were God's men. Paul is going to write to them about this. He is going to show them that the centrality of Christ is the answer to the factions and fractures in the church. My friend, there will be no solution until men and women are willing to come to the person of Christ.

In addition to the three groups, a fourth group was saying, "We are of Christ." They were not actually putting Christ first, but they were the super-duper spiritual group. It is my private opinion that this was the worst group of all. They made a little cult of Christ. They had their little clique in the church, and they excluded other believers. They were the spiritual snobs.

Do you realize that you and I are living in a day when the church has been destroyed from the inside? The problems are not on the outside today. Innumerable churches have long since been destroyed by liberals in the pulpit. Go around on Sunday night or at midweek service and see what the attendance is. Many churches are destroyed by the man in the pulpit. If the man in the pulpit is sound in the faith, you'll find troublemakers in the pew. That is where strife is stirred up. This does more damage to the cause of Christ than alcohol or atheism or worldliness. In many churches they are doing what they did in the mountains of Kentucky and Tennessee; they're feudin' and fussin' like the Martins and the Coys.

Oh, the Martins and the Coys,
    They was reckless mountain boys,
And they took up fam'ly feudin' when they'd meet.

They would shoot each other quicker
Than it took your eye to flicker.
They could knock a squirrel's eye at ninety feet.

Oh, the Martins and the Coys,
   They was reckless mountain boys,
But old Abel Martin was the next to go.
   Though he saw the Coys a-comin'
   He had hardly started runnin'
'Fore a volley shook the hills and laid him low.

After that they started out to fight in earnest
   And they scarred the mountains up with shot
      and shell.
   There was uncles, brothers, cousins,
   They say they bumped them off by dozens,
Just how many bit the dust is hard to tell.

Oh, the Martins and the Coys,
   They was reckless mountain boys,
At the art of killin' they became quite deft.
   They all knowed they shouldn't do it,
   But before they hardly knew it,
On each side they only had one person left.
                    "The Martins and the Coys"
                    —Ted Weems and Al Cameron

This may sound corny and very silly, but unfortunately feudin'
and fussin' go on inside churches. This is what they were doing in the
Corinthian church. Now Paul tackles this problem. He asks,

**Is Christ divided? was Paul crucified for you? or were ye
baptized in the name of Paul? [1 Cor. 1:13].**

The answer is obvious. Of course, Christ is not divided. Anything
that breaks up the unity in Christ has something wrong with it—
regardless of what it is. The crucifixion of Christ is the bedrock of

Christian unity, and it is absurd to contemplate establishing a unity on any other basis.

"Were ye baptized in the name of Paul?" In this instance I do not believe Paul is referring to water baptism, which was always in the name of the Father, Son, and Holy Spirit. Rather, he is referring to the baptism of the Holy Spirit. His question is: "Were ye baptized in the name of Paul?" They would have to say, "Of course not! We weren't baptized in your name. The baptism that placed us in the body of Christ was the baptism of the Holy Spirit. No man could do that for us." You see, Paul is attempting to direct their thinking away from man and back to Christ. They needed to be occupied with the person of Christ. Very candidly, I have always been able to fellowship with any man, regardless of his label, if he can meet with me around the person of Christ.

I thank God that I baptized none of you, but Crispus and Gaius;

Lest any should say that I had baptized in mine own name [1 Cor. 1:14–15].

Here he is talking about water baptism. He is saying that he didn't specialize even in that because of the danger of folk thinking that he was baptizing in his own name. You see, he is focusing on the centrality of Christ. There are folk even in our day who think that water baptism saves them or that it actually has some mystical power that cannot be gotten otherwise.

And I baptized also the household of Stephanas: besides, I know not whether I baptized any other [1 Cor. 1:16].

Paul attached so little importance to baptism that he couldn't really remember whether he had baptized anyone else or not.

For Christ sent me not to baptize, but to preach the gospel: not with wisdom of words, lest the cross of Christ should be made of none effect [1 Cor. 1:17].

It is important for us to see today that there are a great many people who are dividing and separating over many secondary issues. This causes schisms and strife in the church. The church in Corinth was fractured by that kind of party spirit. Three men, Apollos, Paul, and Cephas, had brought to Corinth a *message* that had a unifying quality and power. The gospel they preached emphasized fusion and not faction. However, because these people were baby Christians, they began to put the emphasis on individuals. Now Paul is drawing their attention away from their factions and their party spirit and turning them to the centrality of Christ.

In the city of Corinth, as well as in many other cities of that day, the emphasis was on philosophy. We shall see this as we move into the chapter.

For the preaching of the cross is to them that perish foolishness; but unto us which are saved it is the power of God [1 Cor. 1:18].

The cross divides men. The cross divides the saved from the unsaved, but it doesn't divide the saved people. It should unite them, you see. A Dutch artist painted a picture called "The Last Judgment." It depicts the throne of God, and away from that throne the lost are falling into space. And as they fall, they *cling together*. This is an accurate picture of the one world that men are working for today. The lost want to come together in one great unity, and they are going to accomplish a great union in the last days. But cutting across the grain of the ecumenical environment and the contemporary thought is the gospel of Christ. The Lord Jesus called Himself a divider of men, and the dividing line is His cross. The preaching of the Cross is to them that perish foolishness; but unto the saved person it is the power of God.

Paul makes it very clear that his method was not in the wisdom of the words of the world, not in the method of dialectics of divisions or differences or opinions or theories, but he just presented the cross of Christ. That brought about a unity of those who were saved. To those who perish, the Cross of Christ is foolishness; but to the saved man it becomes the power of God. The Cross of Christ divides the world, but it does not divide the church.

For it is written, I will destroy the wisdom of the wise, and will bring to nothing the understanding of the prudent.

Where is the wise? where is the scribe? where is the disputer of this world? hath not God made foolish the wisdom of this world?

For after that in the wisdom of God the world by wisdom knew not God, it pleased God by the foolishness of preaching to save them that believe [1 Cor. 1:19-21].

Notice that it is not foolish preaching but the foolishness of preaching.

For the Jews require a sign, and the Greeks seek after wisdom:

But we preach Christ crucified, unto the Jews a stumblingblock, and unto the Greeks foolishness [1 Cor. 1:22-23].

Notice that Paul divides mankind into two great ethnic groups: the Jews and the Greeks (meaning Gentiles). He recognizes this twofold division. The Jew represented religion. He had a God-given religion. The Jews felt that they had the truth, and they did—as far as the Old Testament was concerned. The problem was that it had become just a ritual to them. They had departed from the Scriptures and followed tradition, which was their interpretation of the Scriptures. The power was gone. Therefore, when Christ appeared, they asked for a sign. Rather than turning to their Scriptures, they asked for a sign. "Then certain of the scribes and of the Pharisees answered, saying, Master, we would see a sign from thee. But he answered and said unto them, An evil and adulterous generation seeketh after a sign; and there shall no sign be given to it, but the sign of the prophet Jonas: For as Jonas was three days and three nights in the whale's belly; so shall the Son of man be three days and three nights in the heart of the earth" (Matt. 12:38-40). The Lord Jesus gave to them the sign of resurrection.

The Greeks were the Gentiles. They represented philosophy. They were the lovers of wisdom. They said they were seeking the truth; they were searching and scanning the universe for truth. They were the rationalists. While the Jews ended up in ritual, the Gentiles ended up as rationalists and had to conform to a pattern of reason.

About four hundred years before Christ came, the Greek nation constructed on the horizon of history a brilliance of mind and artistic accomplishment of such dimensions that it still dazzles and startles mankind. It continued for about three centuries. By the time of Christ, the glory of Greece was gone. It just fizzled out. There were men like Pericles, Anaxagoras, Thales, Socrates, Plato, and Aristotle who left certain schools such as the Epicurean school, the Stoic school of philosophy, and the Peripatetic school. Then they all disappeared.

There followed two thousand years of philosophical sterility and stagnation in the world. Then there appeared men like Bacon, Hobbes, and Descartes, and there was a rebirth of great thinkers for a brief period of brilliance. This was again followed by decadence, and we are still in it today—even though some of our boys think they are very smart.

"What is truth?" asked the fatalistic Pilate. Bacon asked the same question, and philosophy is still asking that question. Philosophy still has no answers to the problems of life. "Where is the wise? where is the scribe? where is the disputer of this world? hath not God made foolish the wisdom of this world?"

Someone has defined philosophy as a blind man in a dark room looking for a black cat that isn't there. The Greeks sought after wisdom. Today man is still searching for some theory or formula, and he thinks that it is through science that he will get the answers to some of the questions of life. Do you think that man today has the answers to the questions of life? I was interested in a statement which I found in a periodical: "The truth is that modern man is overimpressed by his own achievements. To put a rocket into an orbit that is more than a hundred miles from the surface of the earth takes a great deal of joint thought and effort, but we tend to overstate the case. Though men who ride a few miles above the earth are called astronauts, this is clearly a misnomer. Men will not be astronauts until they ride among the stars, and it is important to remember that most of the stars are thousands of light-years away. The Russians are even more unrestrained in their overstatements, calling their men cosmonauts. Someone needs to say, 'Little man, don't take yourself quite so seriously.'"

Man today thinks he has a few answers. Where are the wise today? It is a good question to ask. You see, God has made foolish the wisdom of this world.

"For after that in the wisdom of God the world by wisdom knew not God, it pleased God by the foolishness of preaching to save them that believe." This is a tremendous statement.

"But we preach Christ crucified, unto the Jews a stumblingblock, and unto the Greeks foolishness." The Jews found the Cross to be a stumblingblock, a *skandalon*. They wanted a sign. They wanted someone to show the way. They wanted a pointer, a highway marker. They would have accepted a deliverer on a white charger who was putting down the power of Rome. But a crucified Christ was an insult to them. That meant *defeat*—not victory. They didn't want to accept that at all. "As it is written, Behold, I lay in Sion a stumblingstone and rock of offence: and whosoever believeth on him shall not be ashamed" (Rom. 9:33). And Peter wrote this: "Unto you therefore which believe he is precious: but unto them which be disobedient, the stone which the builders disallowed, the same is made the head of the corner, And a stone of stumbling, and a rock of offence, even to them which stumble at the word, being disobedient: whereunto also they were appointed" (1 Pet. 2:7-8). A crucified Christ was a stumblingblock to the Jew.

To the Greeks (or Gentiles) the Cross was foolishness, an absurdity. They considered it utterly preposterous and ridiculous and contrary to any rational, worldly system. In Rome there has been found a caricature of Christianity, a figure on the cross with an ass' head. Also in our day our Savior is being ridiculed.

Now Paul bears down on philosophy. While he was in the city of Corinth, he was preaching Christ. "And when they opposed themselves, and blasphemed, he shook his raiment, and said unto them, Your blood be upon your own heads; I am clean: from henceforth I will go unto the Gentiles" (Acts 18:6). Can philosophy lift man out of the cesspool of this life? It never has. Notice that men will be saved, not by foolish preaching, but by the preaching of "foolishness," that is, by the preaching of the Cross. It is not the method but the message that the natural man considers foolish. Men still reject it. Today the wisdom of the world is to have an antipoverty program or some other kind of program. Or the wisdom of the world is to save man from his problems by education. May I say that what man needs today is the gospel. The wisdom of the world has never considered that.

Now Paul introduces another class of mankind. "Unto them which are called, both Jews and Greeks"—these are the called, the elect. They have not only heard the invitation, they have responded to it. And they have found in the Cross of Christ the wisdom and power of God which has transformed their lives, made them new men. The Lord Jesus molded eleven men, then called Saul of Tarsus, and sent them out. They took the gospel to Corinth with its sin, to Ephesus with its religion. For over nineteen hundred years the gospel has been going around the world, and it is the only help and the only hope of mankind.

> **But unto them which are called, both Jews and Greeks, Christ the power of God, and the wisdom of God.**

> **Because the foolishness of God is wiser than men; and the weakness of God is stronger than men.**

> **For ye see your calling, brethren, how that not many wise men after the flesh, not many mighty, not many noble, are called [1 Cor. 1:24–26].**

Some folk like to give emphasis to the prominent folk who have accepted Christ—the entertainment greats, the leaders in industry, and the prominent in government. But God majors in average people. He is calling simple folk like you and me.

> **But God hath chosen the foolish things of the world to confound the wise; and God hath chosen the weak things of the world to confound the things which are mighty [1 Cor. 1:27].**

This does not mean these men are foolish. It means they seem foolish to the world. They are not weak; they are weak in the estimation of the world. This is God's method. He even chooses the base.

And base things of the world, and things which are despised, hath God chosen, yea, and things which are not, to bring to nought things that are:

That no flesh should glory in his presence [1 Cor. 1:28–29].

We do not have a thing to glory about.

But of him are ye in Christ Jesus, who of God is made unto us wisdom, and righteousness, and sanctification, and redemption [1 Cor. 1:30].

Oh, my friend, He is everything that we need. I wish I could get that over to you. He has been made to us wisdom. He is our righteousness. He is our sanctification and our redemption. Whatever it is that you need today, you will find it in Him.

That, according as it is written, He that glorieth, let him glory in the Lord [1 Cor. 1:31].

Our glory should be in the Lord. We should glory in the Lord Jesus Christ today. Let me ask you, what do you glory in? What are you boasting of today? Are you boasting of your degrees? Of your wisdom? Of your wealth? Of your power? Are you boasting today of your position and your character? My friend, you don't have a thing of which you can boast—and I know I haven't. But we can boast of Christ. *He* is everything. He is everything that we need.

CHAPTER 2

THEME: *The clarity of the Holy Spirit corrects human wisdom*

And I, brethren, when I came to you, came not with excellency of speech or of wisdom, declaring unto you the testimony of God [1 Cor. 2:1].

First, I would like to call your attention to the fact that Paul did not use the philosophic method of preaching. He was not a textual or a topical preacher; he was an expositor of the Word of God. I personally believe that is God's method. It was the method our Lord used, by the way. Neither did Paul use flowery nor oratorical language.

Secondly, Paul did not come in the wisdom of the world, declaring the testimony or the *mystery* of God. What does he mean by a mystery? We will be confronted with this word again in the epistle. A mystery simply means "that which had not been revealed before." The mystery of God which Paul preached was that Jesus Christ had been crucified. That had not been preached before but now had been revealed. In the Old Testament the crucifixion of Christ was revealed in type and in prophecy only. The actual event was something new, something not previously revealed.

For I determined not to know any thing among you, save Jesus Christ, and him crucified [1 Cor. 2:2].

Paul did not enter into philosophical discussions that gender strife. He simply stayed right with the preaching of the Cross of Christ. He preached a crucified Savior, One who had died for the sins of the world. That is the type of ministry which is so desperately needed today.

And I was with you in weakness, and in fear, and in much trembling [1 Cor. 2:3].

Paul opens his heart and lets us see his inmost thoughts. He makes it very clear that while he was among them he was greatly disturbed. He was "in weakness, and in fear, and in much trembling." Little wonder that he could say that God had chosen the weak things of this world. Paul had no exalted conception of himself; yet he was a great intellect and a great man in many ways. Obviously, he never thought of himself as great.

> **And my speech and my preaching was not with enticing words of man's wisdom, but in demonstration of the Spirit and of power [1 Cor. 2:4].**

In our day we have a great many words of man's wisdom. There is a great deal of preaching, but very little of it is done "in demonstration of the Spirit and of power." The feeling is that we only need the right method or the right topic or the right style. Oh, how we need the power of the Holy Spirit in our preaching!

> **That your faith should not stand in the wisdom of men, but in the power of God [1 Cor. 2:5].**

In other words, if human wisdom is used to win a man, then his faith stands on human wisdom. If a man is brought to faith through the power of God, then his faith rests upon that. This is the reason I sincerely question a great deal of this apologetic preaching today—such as trying to prove that the Bible is God's Word or that the first chapter of Genesis is scientific or that the Flood really happened. Don't misunderstand me, there is a place for that, and I thank God for men who have specialized in those areas. But we need to understand that salvation does not rest upon whether we can actually prove the inspiration of Scripture, although I certainly believe we can prove it. The question is: What does your faith rest upon? Apologetic preaching will call our attention to the Word of God, but our faith must rest on the power of God.

> Howbeit we speak wisdom among them that are perfect:
> yet not the wisdom of this world, nor of the princes of
> this world, that come to nought [1 Cor. 2:6].

Paul says, "I do not use the worldly methods at all."

> But we speak the wisdom of God in a mystery, even the
> hidden wisdom, which God ordained before the world
> unto our glory [1 Cor. 2:7].

Again here is this word *mystery*. Let's be clear on this word. It has no reference to what we commonly think of as an enigma or with a "who-done-it"—that is, a story dealing with the solution of a mysterious crime. It is not something of a secretive quality or character. The word *mystery*, as used in the Scriptures, refers to something which was not known in the past but is now revealed. This word occurs about twenty-seven times in the New Testament. Our Lord used it when He said "Because it is given unto you to know the mysteries of the kingdom of heaven . . ." (Matt. 13:11). The parables that follow in Matthew 13 are the "mystery parables." Why are they called the mystery parables? It is because in them Jesus explains the direction that the kingdom is going to take in the interval between the rejection of the King and the time when He comes to set up His Kingdom. That segment of history was actually not revealed in the Old Testament at all. God had not yet revealed that to men. When Jesus spoke the mystery parables in Matthew 13, He was revealing this for the first time. What had been previously hidden, Jesus revealed.

Now here in the Epistle to the Corinthians, Paul says, "God's wisdom in a mystery." This is quite interesting because it is a word that came out of Greek schools of philosophy, of the occult, and of science. Paul fastens on this Greek word, and he says, "We speak God's wisdom in a mystery," but he gives it an entirely new meaning. *Mystery* comes from the word meaning "mouth," and it means to shut the mouth—it is something secretive. However, Paul never used it in that way. Rather, that which had been silent has now become vocal. That which had not been known and *could* not be known by human investigation now is known. "Mystery" in the New Testament always means something undiscoverable by the activity of the human intellect but is revealed so that human intellect can apprehend it.

"We speak the wisdom of God"—Paul says, "We have a philosophy." It is not of this age, not of this world, but it is *God's* wisdom, and it pertains to the Cross of Christ. "We speak the wisdom of God in a mystery, even the hidden wisdom, which God ordained before the world unto our glory."

> **Which none of the princes of this world knew: for had they known it, they would not have crucified the Lord of glory [1 Cor. 2:8].**

You see, they did not know.

> **But as it is written, Eye hath not seen, nor ear heard, neither have entered into the heart of man, the things which God hath prepared for them that love him [1 Cor. 2:9].**

This verse surely has been misunderstood. It has gone to a funeral too many times. This is a verse that should never go to a funeral. It has been wrongly used so many times to imply: Here lies dear Mr. So-and-So. His remains are here before us. In this life he didn't understand too well, but now he is in glory and he understands all things. This is not what Paul intended this verse to convey! Paul is saying that right here and now there are certain things that the eye has not seen. We get a great deal of information through the eye-gate. We learn more through our eye-gate than we do in any other way. Another way we gain human wisdom is through the ear-gate. We certainly learn by hearing. Paul says there are certain things we simply cannot learn by hearing. Then he says, "neither have entered into the heart of man," that is, by cogitation, thinking, or reasoning. There are certain things which cannot be attained by human means. You cannot discover God by searching for Him. The things which God has prepared for them who love Him are not gotten through the eye-gate, the ear-gate, or by reasoning. Then how are you going to get them?

> **But God hath revealed them unto us by his Spirit: for the Spirit searcheth all things, yea, the deep things of God [1 Cor. 2:10].**

What we cannot get through the eye-gate or the ear-gate, the Spirit of God can teach us. There are many things we can learn by studying the Bible—such as the history of it, the poetry of it—but we cannot get spiritual truths that way. Why? Because "God hath revealed them unto us by His Spirit." There are certain things that only the Spirit of God can reveal to us.

> **For what man knoweth the things of a man, save the spirit of man which is in him? even so the things of God knoweth no man, but the Spirit of God [1 Cor. 2:11].**

You and I can understand each other because we have human spirits. For instance, I know how you feel when you fall down. It's embarrassing, isn't it? One snowy morning in Nashville I watched an elder of my church come out of his house with two scuttles full of ashes that he was taking out to the alleyway to dump into his garbage can. He slipped and fell, but he held onto the scuttles. He didn't spill an ash, but he really fell hard. He got up and looked all over the landscape to see if anybody had watched him. Why did he do that? He was embarrassed. I knew exactly how he felt because it sure did look funny and I couldn't help but laugh. Because I have the spirit of man and he has the spirit of man, I knew exactly how he felt. However, I do not know how God feels. If I am to understand anything about God, He will have to reveal it to me.

> **Now we have received, not the spirit of the world, but the spirit which is of God; that we might know the things that are freely given to us of God [1 Cor. 2:12].**

There are certain things that we can understand only if the Spirit of God reveals them to us, and He does this freely. He *wants* to be our Teacher!

Which things also we speak, not in the words which man's wisdom teacheth, but which the Holy Ghost teacheth; comparing spiritual things with spiritual [1 Cor. 2:13].

Now Paul will make a very profound statement, and it is one of the axioms of Scripture.

But the natural man receiveth not the things of the Spirit of God: for they are foolishness unto him: neither can he know them, because they are spiritually discerned [1 Cor. 2:14].

The natural man cannot receive the things of God. Why not? Because they are foolishness to him. If you are not a Christian, my friend, what I am saying seems foolish to you. If it doesn't, there is something wrong with you or there is something wrong with me—one of us is wrong. God says the natural man finds the preaching of the Cross of Christ for salvation foolish. It simply does not make sense to him.

"Neither can he know them." When I was a student in college, I had the high-minded notion that anything that any man wrote I could understand. Well, I have found that isn't true. Certainly I cannot understand the Word of God until the Spirit of God opens my heart and mind to understand. It is spiritually discerned. Only the Spirit of God can take the things of Christ and show them unto us. The Lord Jesus said that: "Howbeit when he, the Spirit of truth, is come, he will guide you into all truth: for he shall not speak of himself; but whatsoever he shall hear, that shall he speak: and he will shew you things to come. He shall glorify me: for he shall receive of mine, and shall shew it unto you" (John 16:13–14). My friend, unless the Spirit of God shows you the things of Christ, this Epistle to the Corinthians will mean very little to you.

But he that is spiritual judgeth all things, yet he himself is judged of no man.

For who hath known the mind of the Lord, that he may instruct him? But we have the mind of Christ [1 Cor. 2:15-16].

"He that is spiritual" is the one who has the Holy Spirit within him; he is a child of God.

He "judgeth all things" means that he understands these things. "Yet he himself is judged of no man" means that he is not understood. The spiritual man is in contrast to the natural man. He understands divine truth, but he is misunderstood by the natural man.

"Who hath known the mind of the Lord, that he may instruct him?" Who can instruct God? Who understands the mind of the Lord? We cannot tell God anything, but God can reveal a great deal to us. However, the Spirit of God cannot reveal spiritual things to us until we have the mind of Christ. If you are not a saved person, don't you really think that the preaching of the Cross is foolishness? Don't you think that a man dying on a cross is totally defeated? Doesn't that impress you more as a bit of foolishness rather than the actual way of salvation? Yet God says that His method and His wisdom was to give His Son to die on the Cross for us in order that we might be saved and that we must put our trust in Him. If you are being honest, I believe you must admit that it does sound foolish.

The other day I read a letter from a man who is a comedian. He says he is a comedian in a nightclub. He listens to me teach the Bible by radio, and he thinks I am an oddball. In fact, he thinks I am funnier than he is! Well, that is the way he *should* feel. Why? Because he is a natural man and cannot discern spiritual things.

You will remember that we labeled this chapter *The clarity of the Holy Spirit corrects human wisdom.* Paul has presented two classes of mankind: the natural man and the spiritual man.

The natural man is the man who is the son of Adam, born into the world with a sinful nature, a propensity to do evil. In fact, that is all the natural man can do. Even when we "do good," we act from mixed motives. (After we become believers, we ought always to search our hearts to see if we are acting from mixed motives, even when we are trying to do the Lord's work.) Paul says that the natural man will not receive the things of the Spirit of God; they are foolishness to him.

Yesterday in the mail I received a letter from a politician, a representative from this area to Washington, D.C. Reading this letter would lead one to think he is going to bring in Utopia and the Millennium altogether. My, he has happy solutions for all the problems of the world! Of course, the opposite party doesn't have the benefit of his vast wisdom and knowledge. When I read his letter through, I had the feeling of keen disappointment. First of all, I know he cannot do what he is saying he will do. Secondly, I realize that he is a natural man. He has no understanding of that which is spiritual. He is not interested in any spiritual solutions to the problems. He thinks he knows how to solve the drug problem, but not in a spiritual way. He promises to solve lawlessness, but not in a spiritual way. He knows no more about spiritual matters than a goat grazing upon grass on the hillside. Years ago it was Gladstone who said that the mark of a great statesman is that he knows the direction God is going to take for the next fifty years. This politician would certainly not qualify by that definition. Actually, we cannot expect too much of the natural man. He will tell you, "I do the very best I can," which is probably an accurate statement.

Then there is the other man, the spiritual man. Paul says that the spiritual man "judgeth all things," meaning he understands, he has a spiritual discernment. His spiritual discernment causes him to be misunderstood by the world because the natural man simply cannot understand why he does the things he does. That is the difference between the spiritual man and the natural man.

You will note that they are the kind of men they are because of their relationship to the Book, the Word of God. To the natural man it is foolishness. The spiritual man discerns the Word of God and recognizes its importance.

CHAPTER 3

THEME: Correct conception of God clarifies Christian
service

As we have seen in chapter 2, Paul has presented two classes of
mankind: the natural man and the spiritual man. Now he makes
a further division, and it is among believers: carnal Christians and
spiritual Christians. Their status as carnal or as spiritual will manifest
itself in their lives and in their Christian service.

> **And I, brethren, could not speak unto you as unto spiri-
> tual, but as unto carnal, even as unto babes in Christ
> [1 Cor. 3:1].**

So here we have the third class. He is the unnatural Christian or the
unnatural man. We learned about the natural man, also we learned
about the spiritual man—whom we can call the supernatural man.
Here we have the unnatural man. He is unnatural because he is a
Christian but is still carnal. He is still a babe in Christ.

In the entire first part of this epistle Paul is speaking about carnalities. In the last part of the epistle he speaks of spiritualities. I think
Paul got very tired of talking about carnalities because, when he
reached chapter 12, you can almost hear him heave a sigh of relief.
And he begins to talk to them about something else: "Now concerning
spiritual gifts, brethren, I would not have you ignorant" (1 Cor. 12:1).

The carnal Christian is the one who hasn't grown up spiritually,
and it is evident that he lacks spiritual discernment—not because he
doesn't have the Holy Spirit dwelling within him, but because he is
not growing in grace and in the knowledge of Christ. Again this is a
consequence of his relationship to the Word of God. That is so important to see. This unnatural man, this carnal Christian, is a babe in
Christ. He has an ability but no desire. A baby has the potential to
become a learned man, but he has to start out by drinking milk. Paul
carries this figure of speech over to the spiritual level.

I have fed you with milk, and not with meat: for hitherto ye were not able to bear it, neither yet now are ye able [1 Cor. 3:2].

Paul cannot talk to such folk about spiritualities. They are not yet ready for it. First he must talk to them about their carnalities. Unfortunately, it is on this level that most church members are living today.

How can we identify the carnal Christian? It is the Christian who is using the weak arm of the flesh. He uses carnal methods to obtain spiritual goals. An obvious example is the kind of Christian who says, "Let's have a banquet or let's put on a musical and introduce some of this modern music." This is carnality.

The Greek word for *carnal* is *sarkikos*, which means "fleshly." In Latin and French the word *carna* means "sensual." We get our word *carnival* from two words, *carne vale*, which means "farewell flesh." You see, carnival was something they had before the season of Lent. During Lent they would practice farewell to the flesh with certain denials of pleasure to the flesh; so just before Lent they would gorge and gourmandize the flesh, get drunk, satisfy and satiate the flesh in every possible way. Then they would be able to do without such things during Lent! An example of this is the Mardi Gras in New Orleans. That literally means "fat Tuesday" and refers to the Tuesday before Lent begins.

Paul described folk like this when he used the expression, ". . . whose God is their belly . . ." (Phil. 3:19). You say, "Oh, that's crude." I agree with you; it is crude. But the thing it speaks about is even more crude. This would be an apt description of a lot of folk. Their motto is: Do what comes naturally. Let the flesh have its way.

Perhaps you are saying, "Well, I'm not a carnal Christian. I don't believe in carnivals—I even get sick on a Ferris wheel. I am a separated Christian." What is the mark of carnality? Paul will tell us here.

For ye are yet carnal: for whereas there is among you envying, and strife, and divisions, are ye not carnal, and walk as men? [1 Cor. 3:3].

You see, the carnal Christian is not necessarily one who rides on roller coasters. It does not mean one who promotes carnivals in his church. What is a carnal Christian? Where do you see him in evidence? Wherever there is strife and division, there is actually a "carnival" going on. In many of the fundamental churches one can see divisions and gossip and strife and bitterness and hatred. When that is going on, we know that the flesh is on display. Sometimes Christians can lose their tempers and cover it over by saying, "Well, I am just being frank." No, they are just being mean, that's all. My friend, you can turn a Sunday school class into a carnival, a missionary society into a carnival, or a prayer meeting into a carnival when you gossip or stir up strife and envy and division.

My friend, you may not do "worldly things," and still you may be a carnal Christian. Listen to Paul:

> For while one saith, I am of Paul; and another, I am of Apollos; are ye not carnal?

> Who then is Paul, and who is Apollos, but ministers by whom ye believed, even as the Lord gave to every man?

> I have planted, Apollos watered; but God gave the increase [1 Cor. 3:4–6].

Paul says, "Both of us are workmen for God." Paul was the one who was the missionary—he had opened up new territory. Apollos came along and held meetings and preached and built up the saints. They were both servants of God.

> So then neither is he that planteth any thing, neither he that watereth; but God that giveth the increase [1 Cor. 3:7].

The important thing is not who the preacher is; the important thing is whether God is using him. If God is using him, then God should have the credit for the results. Give God the praise and the glory.

> Now he that planteth and he that watereth are one: and
> every man shall receive his own reward according to his
> own labour [1 Cor. 3:8].

We need to recognize that God uses many workmen. They may each be doing things a little bit differently. That is why we should not go into a tirade against any individual whom the Lord is using. There are many men who use different methods. Many men do things in a different way from the way I would do them. Yet God uses these men. We are all workmen together with God.

> For we are labourers together with God: ye are God's
> husbandry, ye are God's building.

> According to the grace of God which is given unto me,
> as a wise masterbuilder, I have laid the foundation, and
> another buildeth thereon. But let every man take heed
> how he buildeth thereupon [1 Cor. 3:9–10].

The foundation was put down over nineteen hundred years ago. You and I cannot put it down. All we can do is to point to that foundation which is Jesus Christ. We can build on that foundation. The important thing is to get out the Word of God and to preach the gospel which alone can save men.

> For other foundation can no man lay than that is laid,
> which is Jesus Christ [1 Cor. 3:11].

Are you building on Him? That is the important question for the believer. When you came to Christ, you came with no works. You came bringing nothing to receive everything! You were put on that Rock which is Christ. Now you can build on that. This is where good works come in.

> Now if any man build upon this foundation gold, silver,
> precious stones, wood, hay, stubble;

> Every man's work shall be made manifest: for the day
> shall declare it, because it shall be revealed by fire; and
> the fire shall try every man's work of what sort it is
> [1 Cor. 3:12–13].

Paul says that you can build on the foundation that has already been laid with six different kinds of material: gold, silver, precious stones, wood, hay, stubble. Fire won't hurt the first three on the list. Actually, the fire purifies gold and silver and precious stones. But fire certainly gets rid of the last three on the list. Wood, hay, and stubble will all disappear into smoke. The believer is at liberty to build on the foundation with any of these materials: gold, silver, precious stones, wood, hay, stubble.

This teaches that the believer can work for a reward. If any man's work abides, work that he has built on the foundation that has already been laid, he shall receive a reward.

> If any man's work abide which he hath built thereupon,
> he shall receive a reward [1 Cor. 3:14].

That is, he shall receive a reward if he is building with gold, silver, or precious stones.

I am of the opinion that we have many wonderful saints of God about us today. I have been able to meet some of these folk—some of them personally and some by letter—whom God is using in a marvelous way. They are building in gold.

As you well know, a little piece of gold isn't as visible as a hay stack. Possibly God is the only One who knows that it is gold. Now a haystack is another thing—I have traveled across flat farmland, and it seemed to me I could see haystacks that were twenty miles away. There are a lot of folk building haystacks, and everybody hears about what they are doing. The haystacks are going to be tested someday, and then there won't be one haystack left because the testing is going to be by fire. The same thing will be true of works of wood or stubble.

If any man's work shall be burned, he shall suffer loss: but he himself shall be saved; yet so as by fire [1 Cor. 3:15].

You see the contrast: "If any man's work abide" which he built on the foundation, he shall receive a reward; if any man's work goes up in smoke, he will suffer a terrible loss, but, he himself will be saved. He does not lose his salvation if he is on the foundation, which is trust in Christ, even though he receives no reward.

Friend, what are you building today? What kind of material are you using? If you are building with gold, it may not be very impressive now. If you are building an old haystack, it will really stand out on the horizon, but it will go up in smoke. I like to put it like this: there are going to be some people in heaven who will be there because their foundation is Christ but who will smell as if they had been bought at a fire sale! Everything they ever did will have gone up in smoke. They will not receive a reward for their works.

Now if you are a carnal Christian, you cannot expect a reward because you have not been rightly related to God through the Word of God. The carnal Christian is the one who does not know the World of God. You see, one can identify the three categories which Paul mentions by their relation to the Word of God. The natural man says it is foolishness. The spiritual man discerns the Word, and it gives him spiritual insight. The carnal Christian says, "Let's have a banquet and not a Bible study." Or he says, "Let's listen to music rather than to the teaching of the Word of God." That is the way you can identify the carnal Christian.

Know ye not that ye are the temple of God, and that the Spirit of God dwelleth in you?

If any man defile the temple of God, him shall God destroy; for the temple of God is holy, which temple ye are [1 Cor. 3:16–17].

The child of God is the temple of the Holy Spirit. Paul will bring this matter to our attention again. Our very bodies belong to Him!

THE BELIEVER POSSESSES ALL THINGS IN CHRIST

Let no man deceive himself. If any man among you seemeth to be wise in this world, let him become a fool, that he may be wise [1 Cor. 3:18].

Unfortunately, most of our seminaries today are trying to train "intellectual" preachers. I have listened to some of them, and very few of them are really intellectual. May I say again that the important thing is to know and preach the Word of God. Oh, if only I could get that across to some of these smart-aleck young fellows in seminary! I have the privilege of speaking in many seminaries today, and I have met so many boys in the seminaries who want to be "intellectual."

For the wisdom of this world is foolishness with God. For it is written, He taketh the wise in their own craftiness.

And again, The Lord knoweth the thoughts of the wise, that they are vain.

Therefore let no man glory in men. For all things are yours;

Whether Paul, or Apollos, or Cephas, or the world, or life, or death, or things present, or things to come; all are yours;

And ye are Christ's; and Christ is God's [1 Cor. 3:19–23].

Oh, how wonderful it is that we do not have to be confined to one narrow group or one particular denomination. Instead of feeling that we belong to so-and-so and can be taught by only one particular teacher or preacher, we can know that all the men of God belong to us. How wonderful! The reason I get along with the Pentecostal brethren is because I know they belong to God. Oh, my friend, those folk belong to me too. And I belong to them. How glorious it is to meet around the person of Christ with other believers who are on the foundation which is Jesus Christ!

CHAPTER 4

THEME: Conditions of Christ's servants constrain Christian conduct

This is the final chapter in which Paul is dealing with the divisions and the party spirit which was in the church in Corinth. In this chapter, he speaks of the conditions of Christ's servants—and that is what should constrain Christian conduct.

Let a man so account of us, as of the ministers of Christ, and stewards of the mysteries of God [1 Cor. 4:1].

Let us pause to look at this wonderful verse. We are all "the ministers of Christ." Every believer is a minister of Christ. Sometimes a member of a congregation will say, "There is my minister." Well, I hope he is rather a minister of Christ because he is responsible to Him. And you, as a minister of Christ, are responsible to Him.

We are all ministers. You are a preacher whether you like it or not. Now don't get angry with me for saying that. There was a man living near our church in Pasadena, when I was pastor there, who was an alcoholic, a real sot. He lived with his mother who was a wonderful Christian lady, and she asked me to talk with him. One day when I saw him staggering down the street, I just sort of detoured him into my study. He sat down and I told him what a sorry fellow he was. He agreed with every bit of it. Then I said to him, "Do you know that you are a preacher?" Well, he stood up and said, "Don't you call me that— I'll hit you!" He didn't mind being called a drunkard or an alcoholic, but he surely didn't want to be called a preacher! Well, we are all preachers. As I told him, "We preach some message by our lives. You are saying something to the world and to those around you by your life. You can't help it. I live my life unto you and you live your life unto me. It's just that way. We have that kind of influence." My friend, if you are a believer, you are a minister of Christ. What kind of message are you giving?

Notice that a minister of Christ is a "steward of the mysteries of God." In Paul's day, a steward was the person who managed the household for the owner. He had charge of the house, the food, the clothing, and that sort of thing. He would give out things to the household as they needed them. Just so, a minister of Christ should dispense the Word of God to the members of the household.

Here we have that word *mystery* again. Remember that mysteries are those things which had not been revealed before but are now made known. The mysteries cannot be understood by the natural man. It is only the Spirit of God who can take the things of Christ and show them to us. The "mystery" here is actually the gospel, the Word of God. Since we are stewards of the "mysteries of God," we are to dispense those mysteries.

After concluding His "mystery parables" in Matthew 13, "Jesus saith unto them, Have ye understood all these things? They say unto him, Yea, Lord" (Matt. 13:51). I'm inclined to think that they didn't really understand at that time; Jesus doesn't say whether or not they understood Him. But He does go on to say to them, ". . . Therefore every scribe which is instructed unto the kingdom of heaven is like unto a man that is an householder, which bringeth forth out of his treasure things new and old" (Matt. 13:52). That is what a steward of the mysteries of God should be doing—bringing forth out of the Word of God things new and things old. Folk sometimes say to me after a Bible study or after a sermon, "That's old. I've heard that before." I answer, "Well, I am a steward to bring forth things both new and old. Today I brought forth a little of the old. It is my business to bring forth the old as well as the new." That is the calling of a steward of the mysteries of God, and I can't think of any calling higher than that.

Moreover it is required in stewards, that a man be found faithful [1 Cor. 4:2].

Notice that it is not required of a steward to be eloquent or to have many gifts, only that he be found faithful. There are so many who will be rewarded someday, not because they did some great thing or had some great gift, but because they were faithful in what they did and how they did it. I learned over the years as a pastor of a church that there were always the faithful few. I could depend on them. And I knew where they stood.

> **But with me it is a very small thing that I should be judged of you, or of man's judgment: yea, I judge not mine own self.**
>
> **For I know nothing by myself; yet am I not hereby justified: but he that judgeth me is the Lord [1 Cor. 4:3–4].**

These two verses actually present the three courts before which we all must appear. They may seem to be rather difficult verses, but actually they are not. They tell us that you have no right to sit in judgment on me, and I have no right to sit in judgment on you because we both are going to stand before a higher court.

1. The first court is the lower court. It is the court of the opinion of others. He says, "But with me it is a very small thing that I should be judged of you, or of man's judgment." Phillips, in his paraphrase, gives an excellent interpretation of this. "But, as a matter of fact, it matters very little to me what you, or any man, thinks of me . . ." (1 Cor. 4:3, PHILLIPS). That is not a literal translation, but it is a good interpretation.

This is a striking statement, and it may sound as if Paul were antisocial. However, Paul was not callous or contemptuous of the opinion of others. He was not immune to the expression and the estimation of those about him. He defended his apostleship with great feeling when he was challenged by his critics. He was always hurt by false rumors. Right here in this very chapter he made mention of it: "Even unto this present hour we both hunger, and thirst, and are naked, and are buffeted, and have no certain dwellingplace; And labour, working with our own hands: being reviled, we bless; being persecuted, we suffer it: Being defamed, we entreat: we are made as the filth of the world, and are the offscouring of all things unto this day" (vv. 11–13). You can see that Paul was very sensitive to the opinions of others; yet his life was not directed by them. They were not at the steering wheel of his life.

Whether we like it or not, we all stand before the judgment seat of others. It is something that we cannot avoid. Abraham Lincoln said, "Public opinion in this country is everything." Unfortunately, it is true. There is a danger to defer to the opinion of others, to yield to the criticism of our enemies and surrender to them. Many of our courts favor the popularity of the crowd instead of justice—certainly the politicians favor the crowd. Some will surrender principles and honor and reputation. John Milton said, "The last infirmity of a noble mind is the love of fame." Unfortunately, that is what many go out to seek today. Horace Greeley of the *New York Tribune* said, "Fame is a vapor, popularity an accident, riches take wings, those who cheer today will curse tomorrow, only one thing endures—character." Someone else has said, "The trouble with most of us is that we would rather be ruined by praise than saved by criticism." I'm afraid that is true also.

Although Paul was sensitive to the opinion of others, that opinion did not become the guiding principle of his life. "With me it is a very small thing that I should be judged of you, or of man's judgment."

2. The second court is a higher court. It is the court of one's own conscience. "Yea, I judge not mine own self."

Is conscience a safe guide? Paul says that it is not an accurate guide. We are to be led of the Spirit. We have already studied about the age of conscience in the Book of Genesis, and there we saw that it ended in the judgment of the Flood. Christians should have an enlightened conscience. When it rebukes us and tells us that we are wrong, we should obey it. However, our conscience can also approve our easygoing ways and can appeal to our vanity and can flatter us. Then we should beware of it. We all stand or fall before this court.

It was Longfellow who put it like this: "Not in the clamor of the crowded street, Not in the shouts and plaudits of the throng, But in ourselves, are triumph and defeat." An honest man will not be guided by the opinion of others, but he will do what he thinks is right. It is a brave formula. It is a noble rule. Yet Paul said that he didn't follow it: ". . . I don't value my opinion of myself . . . but that doesn't justify me before God" (1 Cor. 4:4, PHILLIPS). It wasn't that Paul knew some bit of evidence against himself. On the contrary, he says he knew nothing against himself, but that still didn't clear him before God. It is characteristic of our human nature to be harsh on others and very lenient with ourselves.

That was David's problem. He could see the evil in someone else, but he couldn't see it in himself. How about us? When others hold tenaciously to some opinion, we call them contentious, but when we do it, we are showing the courage of our convictions. Others cause divisions and make trouble, but we are standing for the right. Others are backslidden when they forsake God's house, but we have a good reason. You know we are not very apt to be severe upon ourselves. We always like to cast ourselves in a leading role, and generally we distort it.

No, we do not stand or fall before ourselves. God may reverse the decision of this second court, the court of our own conscience.

3. There is a third court before which we must stand—"he that judgeth me is the Lord." The supreme court is of the one and only Master; it is the *bēma* or the judgment seat of Christ. Paul says that he is going to stand someday before the judgment seat of Christ. Each one of us will appear before that judgment seat. (He will say more about this in chapter 5 of his Second Epistle to the Corinthians.)

What is going to be judged there? We know that we shall not be judged for our sins because a believer's sins have been removed as far as the east is from the west (see Ps. 103:12). Our sins are under the blood of Jesus Christ and God remembers them no more. The believer will be judged for his stewardship. All our physical possessions—our bodies, our material resources, our giving—these are the things that will be brought up for judgment. So you can see that being a faithful steward is very important.

After all, we own nothing. We have learned before that all things are Christ's and that we belong to Him. We are in partnership with Him. We saw at the close of chapter 3 that all things are ours. Paul is ours and Apollos is ours. Calvin is ours and John Wesley is ours and Martin Luther is ours. This world we live in is ours—we can enjoy the beauty of its scenery, the mountains, the trees, the ocean, and life itself. (I wouldn't want to be dead today, would you?) But even death is ours! Dr. Parker says, "Death is yours. It belongs to you. Death is not to master you, you are going to master it." Death is yours. How wonderful that is. When we belong to Christ, all things are ours—present and future. And we are stewards of all He has entrusted to us.

Therefore judge nothing before the time, until the Lord come, who both will bring to light the hidden things of darkness, and will make manifest the counsels of the hearts: and then shall every man have praise of God [1 Cor. 4:5].

He is the One who will judge. If we sit in judgment on someone else, we are taking the Lord's place. This is why we need not react to insult or criticism by fighting back. God will judge us fairly, and He knows all the facts. (Anyway, we probably know worse things about ourselves than does the person who is criticizing us!) The hidden works of darkness are going to be brought out into the light in the presence of Jesus Christ. He will make manifest the counsels of the hearts. This is why we should be very careful how we live today.

Then there is this remarkable statement: "then shall every man have praise of God." I believe that He is going to find something for which He can *praise* every saint of God.

In the Book of Revelation Christ has a word of commendation for each of the seven churches of Asia Minor—with the exception of Laodicea, which probably was not really His church anyway. He had words of commendation for the churches in spite of their faults. And I think He will be equally gracious to each individual saint.

A dear little lady in a church years ago always had something good to say about everybody, especially the preacher. One day they had a visiting preacher who delivered the most miserable sermon they had ever heard. The people wondered what in the world the dear little lady would say about such a sermon, and they gathered round as she went out. She smiled and shook hands with the preacher, then she said, "Oh, pastor, you had a wonderful *text* today!" And, my friend, I think our Lord is going to find something praiseworthy in each of us!

THE APPLICATION

And these things, brethren, I have in a figure transferred to myself and to Apollos for your sakes; that ye might learn in us not to think of men above that which is written, that no one of you be puffed up for one against another [1 Cor. 4:6].

Remember that one of the problems in the Corinthian church was divisions. So now Paul says that he is using this for an illustration for them. Paul and Apollos were friends; they both belonged to Christ, and Christ belonged to both of them. Both men were exercising their gifts.

For who maketh thee to differ from another? and what hast thou that thou didst not receive? now if thou didst receive it, why dost thou glory, as if thou hadst not received it? [1 Cor. 4:7].

Do you have a gift? You may have a very outstanding gift, but you have nothing to boast about because God gave it to you. You are not the originator of your gift. We ought to thank God for our gifts.

Now ye are full, now ye are rich, ye have reigned as kings without us: and I would to God ye did reign, that we also might reign with you.

For I think that God hath set forth us the apostles last, as it were appointed to death: for we are made a spectacle unto the world, and to angels, and to men [1 Cor. 4:8-9].

The apostles in that great martyr period of the church have been set before the world as a spectacle. Not only are they a spectacle to the world but also to angels and to men—and I think that refers to us today. Other men have labored, my friend, and we have entered into their labors.

Now Paul will tell us what he had gone through in order that we might have this epistle and be enjoying the study of it right now.

We are fools for Christ's sake, but ye are wise in Christ; we are weak, but ye are strong; ye are honourable, but we are despised.

Even unto this present hour we both hunger, and thirst, and are naked, and are buffeted, and have no certain dwellingplace;

And labour, working with our own hands: being reviled, we bless; being persecuted, we suffer it:

Being defamed, we entreat: we are made as the filth of the world, and are the offscouring of all things unto this day [1 Cor. 4:10–13].

You and I can't imagine how the apostle Paul suffered in order to get out the gospel of Jesus Christ. He *evangelized* Asia Minor. We are told that in the province of Asia everyone, both Jew and Gentile, heard the Word of God!

I write not these things to shame you, but as my beloved sons I warn you.

For though ye have ten thousand instructors in Christ, yet have ye not many fathers: for in Christ Jesus I have begotten you through the gospel [1 Cor. 4:14–15].

Paul was the missionary who led them to Christ. It is a wonderful thing to be the spiritual father of someone whom you have led to Christ.

For this cause have I sent unto you Timotheus, who is my beloved son, and faithful in the Lord, who shall

> bring you into remembrance of my ways which be in
> Christ, as I teach every where in every church [1 Cor.
> 4:17].

We see here the personal esteem Paul had for Timothy.

> Now some are puffed up, as though I would not come to
> you.
>
> But I will come to you shortly, if the Lord will, and will
> know, not the speech of them which are puffed up, but
> the power.
>
> For the kingdom of God is not in word, but in power
> [1 Cor. 4:18–20].

Paul says that he is not so much interested in their talk, but he wants
to know whether or not there is power in their lives.

> What will ye? shall I come unto you with a rod, or in
> love, and in the spirit of meekness? [1 Cor. 4:21].

Their attitude and action will determine how Paul shall come to them.
Will he need to come with a "rod" of correction, or can he come in
love and in a spirit of meekness?

CHAPTERS 5 AND 6

THEME: Scandals in the Corinthian church

IMPURITY

It is reported commonly that there is fornication among you, and such fornication as is not so much as named among the Gentiles, that one should have his father's wife [1 Cor. 5:1].

This was a case that was up before the church. This was not gossip. It could be translated: "It is reported actually and factually." This was not just a rumor that was going around. This case was common knowledge. It was such fornication that was not even mentioned among the Gentiles. It was the sordid story of a man who took his father's wife, his own stepmother.

And ye are puffed up, and have not rather mourned, that he that hath done this deed might be taken away from among you [1 Cor. 5:2].

The apostle is using strong language here. He is dealing with a very grievous sin. The congregation in Corinth was compromising with this evil.

We need to recognize that flagrant sin in the church must be dealt with. The Lord Jesus had given detailed instructions in Matthew 18: "Moreover if thy brother shall trespass against thee, go and tell him his fault between thee and him alone: if he shall hear thee, thou hast gained thy brother. But if he will not hear thee, then take with thee one or two more, that in the mouth of two or three witnesses every word may be established. And if he shall neglect to hear them, tell it unto the church: but if he neglect to hear the church, let him be unto thee as an heathen man and a publican" (Matt. 18:15–17).

They did not carry out this procedure in Corinth. This was a case of compromise with evil. John Morley has said that compromise is the most immoral word in the English language. I think I would agree to that. The church in Corinth was compromising itself by compromising with this evil.

There are certain things about this case that we need to note. This case was an acknowledged situation which had no need of proof. This was not a matter of gossip or of hearsay. Paul would never have brought up something like this if it had simply been a rumor.

Also we need to note that it was not a questionable sin. It was a glaring sin, and it was actually recognized by the world outside as being sin. It was incest. This is in contrast to questionable activities, which should not be brought out in the open and dealt with by the church. Let me give an illustration of what I mean.

A lady was converted in the church where I served as pastor. She called me one day about three months after her conversion, and she was very disturbed. She said, "I'm very disappointed and very discouraged. I have been a chain smoker and have wanted to give up cigarettes. I have tried for three months and I have failed. I have come to the place where I hate them and I hate myself for not being able to give them up. What should I do?" I gave her several suggestions. I said, "Look, it is a questionable sin, and it is one that you hate and want to give up. I don't blame you; your testimony is involved. First of all, continue to pray, and ask your personal friends to continue to pray for you, as you say they are doing. Also I will pray for you. I know God will give you the victory because you want it. Secondly, don't be discouraged. And the third thing is: please do not tell it to the dear saints in the church. If you do, they will absolutely skin you alive because they consider it the worst sin in the world." After about three months I saw her coming into the church, and I could tell by her face something had happened. After the service she could hardly wait to talk to me. She said, "I have wonderful news for you. From the day I talked to you down to the present, I haven't smoked once. God has given me deliverance!"

Now, smoking is one of the things I classify as a questionable sin. It is not mentioned in the Word of God; nor does it have any question of immorality connected with it. Therefore, it is to be handled differently. It is not to be brought before the church for judgment. By contrast, this case of immorality in the Corinthian church was a flaunting of God's law. Therefore, this needed to be handled with church discipline. There was no doubt about this being a sin. It is not a questionable matter. It was such a horrible sin that it was not even practiced by the Gentiles outside the church.

I would like to say something to our present generation. Living together without being married is sin in God's sight. It makes no difference what public opinion says about it or how many people are practicing it. The Word of God calls this sin, and there is no other way one can look at it. It is not a questionable sin as far as the Word of God is concerned.

The church in Corinth did not need to establish the fact that the man was living in sin. Their error was that they tolerated it. They condoned the sin by doing nothing about it. They compromised, and that is the worst thing they could have done. You can put this down as an axiom: A pure church is a powerful church; an impure church is a paralyzed church. You can look around you at churches today and see whether or not that is true.

> **For I verily, as absent in body, but present in spirit, have judged already, as though I were present, concerning him that hath so done this deed,**
>
> **In the name of our Lord Jesus Christ, when ye are gathered together, and my spirit, with the power of our Lord Jesus Christ,**
>
> **To deliver such an one unto Satan for the destruction of the flesh, that the spirit may be saved in the day of the Lord Jesus [1 Cor. 5:3–5].**

Paul is telling them to meet together, and if this brother will not forsake his sin, they are to deliver him over to Satan. That is a tremendous statement. Does he really mean that? He said it; apparently he meant it.

This is something that the Word of God teaches. Do you remember that Job was delivered over to Satan? Satan came to the Lord and complained that He wouldn't let him touch Job. He told God in effect, "You tell me how good a man Job is, but if You will just let me get to him, I will show You whether or not Job really is true to You. He will curse You to Your face!" So the Lord gave Satan permission to test Job—with the limitation that he could not take Job's life. There is a great comfort in this for us: Satan cannot touch a child of God unless he has the permission of God Himself. And if God does permit it, then it is for a reason.

You will also remember that the Lord Jesus told Peter that Satan desired to have him to sift him as wheat. The Lord Jesus permitted Satan to do this to Peter. Peter was turned over to Satan, and that night he denied his Lord. What he did was just as dastardly as the crime of Judas Iscariot. However, Peter hated himself and he hated what he had done, but it taught him how weak he was. God used this experience to produce the kind of man who would get up and preach the sermon that Peter preached on the Day of Pentecost.

Then there is the example in 1 Timothy 1:20 where Paul writes: "Of whom is Hymenaeus and Alexander; whom I have delivered unto Satan, that they may learn not to blaspheme." These two men were professing Christians, but they were blaspheming. Paul says he delivered them over to Satan.

Now I realize there is danger of our feelings and our emotions getting involved, and there is a danger of fanaticism to which some people are inclined; but in our churches today we do have certain men and women who are hurting the cause of Christ. I believe we have the right to ask God to deliver them into the hands of Satan, to be dealt with, so that they won't hurt and harm the body of Christ. I pray that God will deliver certain men over to Satan to let him give them a good workout. It will either bring them to God (if they are true believers) or it will reveal the fact that they are not genuine believers at all. If they are Christians, then they will come out clear-cut and come out clean for God and for the Lord Jesus Christ. I think we have a right to pray that prayer.

This is strong medicine! And for these carnal Corinthians it was strong medicine. Paul is writing that, although he can't be with them in his body, he is with them in his spirit. He tells them the way he is voting. And his prayer is to deliver this man into the hands of Satan.

Your glorying is not good. Know ye not that a little leaven leaveneth the whole lump? [1 Cor. 5:6].

Do you know what the church in Corinth was doing? At the same time that they were shutting their eyes to the sin that was in their own congregation, they were bragging about their other activities. They were glorying—boasting. Probably they bragged about the missionaries they sent out and about being true to the Scriptures and about winning souls for Christ. What hypocrisy! Yet there are many folk who feel that being busy in Christian work covers a multitude of sins. Paul says that their glorying was not good. Didn't they know that a little leaven leavens the whole lump? Leaven is never a symbol of the gospel; it is always a principle of evil, and it represents evil in this instance.

Purge out therefore the old leaven, that ye may be a new lump, as ye are unleavened. For even Christ our passover is sacrificed for us [1 Cor. 5:7].

What does leaven do to the bread? Well, you put it in the dough, set it in a warm place, and the bread begins to puff up. When it gets to a certain height, the bread is put into the hot oven. Why? To stop the leavening process. If the bread did not get into the oven, that leavening process would go on and the bread would rise higher and higher. Finally the whole loaf would be corrupt and rotten. Now that is exactly what happens with evil in the church if it is not dealt with. Finally the whole thing will blow up and will destroy the effectiveness of the church. A little leaven will leaven the whole lump; so it must be purged out.

In the Old Testament, after the Feast of the Passover there followed immediately the Feast of Unleavened Bread. Paul says that Christ, the true Passover Lamb, has now been sacrificed for us. This should be followed by lives that are free from leaven. Instead, this Corinthian congregation was allowing leaven—that is, evil—to come right into their church. These were the very ones who were talking about the death of Christ and the crucifixion of Christ, and yet they permitted leaven to enter into the church.

Therefore let us keep the feast, not with old leaven, neither with the leaven of malice and wickedness; but with the unleavened bread of sincerity and truth [1 Cor. 5:8].

Paul is not talking about how a person is saved. He is talking about the walk of the believer after he has been saved. Sincerity never saved anyone. But if you are a child of God, you will be sincere. The world today needs to see sincerity among believers and needs truth among believers. Paul says, "Let's have sincerity and truth in the church there in Corinth." You see, the church there was really insincere. They had gross immorality in their midst. They thought they could get by with this, and they pretended that everything was all right. They were pretending that they were telling the truth and living the truth when actually they were not.

I wrote unto you in an epistle not to company with fornicators:

Yet not altogether with the fornicators of this world, or with the covetous, or extortioners, or with idolaters; for then must ye needs go out of the world.

But now I have written unto you not to keep company, if any man that is called a brother be a fornicator, or covetous, or an idolater, or a railer, or a drunkard, or an extortioner; with such an one no not to eat [1 Cor. 5:9–11].

Paul had previously written to them and had condemned these sins. Corinth was a city given over to immorality. There were a thousand priestesses at the temple of Venus or Aphrodite who were nothing in the world but harlots. They were prostitutes, and the whole city was given over to this immorality in the name of religion. Now here they are permitting this immoral man to come into their fellowship and to eat with them. They patted him on the back and accepted him as one of their own when they knew he was living in sin. The church in Corinth thought they could drop down to the level of the world.

Does the church today think it can drop down to the immorality of the world and get away with it? My friend, the church today has lost its power. I am speaking of the church in general. Thank God there are still wonderful churches left, churches that stand out like beacon lights across this land, Bible churches that stand for the Word of God. The other day I heard of a young preacher who took a stand when they tried to introduce hard rock music into his church. It meant that he lost several hundred of his members who walked out. I thank God for a preacher like that, one with intestinal fortitude. Most men today are compromising and shutting their eyes and letting the world come in. The church has lost its power. An impure church is a paralyzed church, and a pure church is a powerful church. That is true for the individual also.

Now Paul says this does not apply to fornication only. He also applies it to covetousness. How about a deacon in the church who has sticky fingers? How about the man in the church who has his hand on a lot of money? Paul also includes idolators, those who are fooling around with other religions. I heard about a leading officer of a church who walked out and joined a cult. I am telling you that the Word of God teaches that a little infection in the church must be dealt with or else it is going to corrupt and wreck the church. A little leaven will leaven the whole lump.

For what have I to do to judge them also that are without? do not ye judge them that are within?

But them that are without God judgeth. Therefore put away from among yourselves that wicked person [1 Cor. 5:12–13].

Paul says that he is not judging the people on the outside. That is not his business. He is to judge those inside the church. God will judge those who are on the outside. It is the business of the church to judge evil which is in the church.

We are interested to know how things worked out in Corinth. To find the answer we need to turn to 2 Corinthians 2:4–8: "For out of much affliction and anguish of heart I wrote unto you with many tears; not that ye should be grieved, but that ye might know the love which I have more abundantly unto you. But if any have caused grief, he hath not grieved me, but in part: that I may not overcharge you all. Sufficient to such a man is this punishment, which was inflicted of many. So that contrariwise ye ought rather to forgive him, and comfort him, lest perhaps such a one should be swallowed up with overmuch sorrow. Wherefore I beseech you that ye would confirm your love toward him."

This immoral man had come in deep repentance after Paul put it down on the line in his previous epistle. Today we need a great deal of courage—not compromise—in the church to point out these things and say, "This is sin." I think that when this is done, the believer who is in sin will confess, like this man in Corinth and like David did, and will repent and change his ways. The Corinthian church handled this very nicely. Why? Because Paul had the courage to write this kind of letter. In 2 Corinthians Paul explains why he had done it: "Wherefore, though I wrote unto you, I did it not for his cause that had done the wrong, nor for his cause that suffered wrong, but that our care for you in the sight of God might appear unto you" (2 Cor. 7:12).

Paul says that he wrote as he did for the welfare of the church of the Lord Jesus Christ. Today we hear this flimsy, hypocritical attitude: "Well, we don't want to air this thing. We don't want to cause trouble. We'll just sweep it under the rug." My friend, God cannot bless a church or an individual that does this. If God did bless, God would be a liar. And you know that God is no liar. He will judge inaction in a case like this.

This chapter has a tremendous lesson for us. And it is very practical, is it not?

LAWSUITS AMONG MEMBERS

Chapter 6 will deal with the subject of the Christian and his relation to the state. The Christian is told that he has a dual citizenship. I think that is often misconstrued by outsiders as well as by believers. Philippians 3:20 states: "For our conversation is in heaven; from whence also we look for the Saviour, the Lord Jesus Christ." The Greek word for "conversation" is *politeuma*, which literally means "Our politics is in heaven; from whence also we look for the Saviour, the Lord Jesus Christ."

His citizenship in heaven does not relieve the Christian of his responsibility to the state. The Christian has a responsibility to each, that is, to God and to the state. Our Lord expressed this when the Herodians pressed on Him the subject of taxation. The Herodians asked, "Tell us therefore, What thinkest thou? Is it lawful to give tribute unto Caesar, or not?" (Matt. 22:17). Jesus answered, ". . . Render therefore unto Caesar the things which are Caesar's; and unto God the things that are God's" (Matt. 22:21). The Christian has a responsibility to the state, and he also has a responsibility to God. The Christian has both secular and spiritual responsibilities.

The apostle Paul defines some very specific responsibilities of Christians to the state. There are certain guidelines which cannot be misunderstood. Paul writes in 1 Timothy 2:1–4: "I exhort therefore, that, first of all, supplications, prayers, intercessions, and giving of thanks, be made for all men; For kings, and for all that are in authority; that we may lead a quiet and peaceable life in all godliness and honesty. For this is good and acceptable in the sight of God our Saviour; Who will have all men to be saved, and to come unto the knowledge of the truth." Our obligation to the state is to attempt to have a peaceful, law-abiding society with recognition of authority. Why is this so important for the Christian? It is in order that we might get out the message of the gospel.

Paul discusses the same subject in Romans 13:1–4: "Let every soul be subject unto the higher powers. For there is no power but of God: the powers that be are ordained of God. Whosoever therefore resisteth the power, resisteth the ordinance of God: and they that resist shall receive to themselves damnation. For rulers are not a terror to good works, but to the evil. Wilt thou then not be afraid of the power? do that which is good, and thou shalt have praise of the same: For he is the minister of God to thee for good. . . ."

This was written at a time when the Roman government was tyrannical. The emperors of that era were dictators, and many of them were persecutors of the church. If anyone tried to oppose the Roman government, he was in real trouble because there was no place to which one could flee where the government could not find him and arrest him. Even in that government, however, there was a freedom to preach the Word of God. That is the thing that Christians should keep in mind.

Back in Genesis we are shown that it was God Himself who ordained the state. As far as I can tell, that has never been changed. God put down this principle: "Whoso sheddeth man's blood, by man shall his blood be shed: for in the image of God made he man" (Gen. 9:6). To maintain the dignity and a respect for humanity, capital punishment must be used.

I have a letter from a very sweet lady who is very softhearted and feels that I am terrible because I believe in capital punishment. She says that Jesus wouldn't do that. She wants to know whether I would be willing to pull the switch at the electric chair. Very candidly, I wouldn't like to do it—that is not my job; I have been called to do something else. But I do want to say this: If this sweet lady wants to be safe in her home, there had better be somebody who is willing to pull that electric switch. We are living in a time of lawlessness. The reason is that we have softhearted judges, and I'm afraid some have been softheaded as well.

The church and the state were to be kept separate. The church was not to dominate the state, not to dictate to it. The state was not to control the church nor to take the place of God. In a secular society, secularism always takes the place of God. That is modern idolatry today. A great many people are putting secularism in the place of God. Someone sent me a modern-day parody on Psalm 23 which begins, "Science is my shepherd, I shall not want." We find the church getting involved in secularism. I have a quotation from a liberal which reads: "To rebel against human law in the name of a higher law can be creative, saving the world from stagnation, but to disobey the law can also be anarchic and destructive, for too easily can men convince themselves that their opinions are those of God." Too many of our statesmen today think they stand in the place of God and that they speak in the place of God.

With that kind of background I think we are prepared to look at chapter 6 of 1 Corinthians. We are still in that division of the epistle which deals with scandals in the Corinthian church. The first was concerned with lawsuits among members.

Dare any of you, having a matter against another, go to law before the unjust, and not before the saints? [1 Cor. 6:1].

This may sound to you like a very strange statement, and it may need some explanation. He does not say that Christians are not to go to law. If Christians did not use the benefit of the law, they would suffer great loss at the hands of the unsaved. He is saying that Christians should not go to law against each other—Christian against Christian. The differences between believers are not to be taken to a secular court. They should be settled by believers. This is something which churches and believers in general ignore today.

After I had come to Southern California as a pastor, I was rather amazed one day when a man came in quite excitedly and wanted to bring a charge against an officer of the church. He claimed this man had beaten him out of a sum of money in a business deal. He said, "Now I want you to bring him up before the board and to make him settle with me." I told him, "I think you are approaching this the right way. When can you appear before the board and make your charges?" "Oh," he said, "I've told you about it. That is all that is necessary." I pointed out to him that I had no way to verify the charge. It would be necessary for both men to appear before the board. Then I asked him, "Would you be willing to accept the verdict of the board?" "Well," he said, "it all depends on how they decided it. If they decided in my favor, I would accept it." So then I asked him if he would accept the verdict if it were against him, and he assured me that he would not. Of course, I told him that we might as well forget the whole matter. I said, "You are not really willing to turn this issue over to other believers for a verdict."

Church fights should not be aired in state courts before unbelievers. Individual differences among Christians should be adjudicated by believers. It is bad enough when two Christian are divorced, but it is an extremely serious matter when Christians go before a secular court and air their differences before unbelievers. When a Christian couple come to me and tell me they simply cannot get along, and I see there is no way of working out a reconciliation, I advise a legal separation, not a court trial.

Why should a believer let other believers be the judges rather than take his case to the unsaved world for their judgment? Again, this does not forbid a Christian from going to court with an unbeliever. Why should two believers bring their differences to be settled by other believers? Paul gives a threefold reason regarding the capabilities of believers to judge.

THE CAPABILITY OF THE BELIEVERS

Do ye not know that the saints shall judge the world? and if the world shall be judged by you, are ye unworthy to judge the smallest matters? [1 Cor. 6:2].

My friend, if you are a believer in Christ, you will have a part with the Lord Jesus in ruling the earth someday. This is not talking about the judgment at the Great White Throne, which will be the judgment when the lost appear before Christ. No, this has to do with the adjudication of the affairs of the universe down through eternity.

1. Saints will judge the world.

The saints shall judge the world. I believe this has to do with what Paul wrote to Timothy, "If we suffer, we shall also reign with him: if we deny him, he also will deny us" (2 Tim. 2:12). I believe this means that we shall pass judgment on the affairs in this world.

Know ye not that we shall judge angels? how much more things that pertain to this life? [1 Cor. 6:3].

2. Saints will judge angels.

Paul is using a series of "know ye nots." When Paul said, "Know ye not," you can be sure that the brethren did not know. This was a polite way of saying they were ignorant of these things.

This certainly opens up a whole new vista of truth. I do not understand what this means; it is beyond my comprehension. All I know is that man was made a little lower than the angels, and through redemption man was lifted into a place of fellowship with God, a position above the angels. Also, God permitted man to fall. He never would have permitted that if it would not work out for good. It will result in bringing man into a higher position. The old bromide is not true that says that the bird with the broken wing never flies so high again. Man flies higher. We are going to be above the angels. We are going to judge them and have charge of them. May I say again, this is beyond my comprehension, but I believe it.

To pick up the third "know ye not," we skip down to verse 9:

Know ye not that the unrighteous shall not inherit the kingdom of God? Be not deceived: neither fornicators, nor idolaters, nor adulterers, nor effeminate, nor abusers of themselves with mankind,

Nor thieves, nor covetous, nor drunkards, nor revilers, nor extortioners, shall inherit the kingdom of God [1 Cor. 6:9–10].

3. Unrighteousness is not in the Kingdom.

Listen very carefully because this is important. No secular judge or jury is equipped to make spiritual decisions because they do not comprehend spiritual principles. That is why court cases that pertain to churches and Christians go haywire the minute they hit the legal mills. A secular judge may know the material in the law books, but he knows nothing about spiritual decisions. He has no spiritual discernment.

To be very candid with you, it would be with fear and trembling that I would go into court and have a secular judge handle me or my property. I don't think a secular judge is capable of doing that, and I don't think a secular jury can either. Following a trial here in Southern California I looked at the jury shown on television and said to my wife, "I thank God my life is not in the hands of the twelve people I see there." After the trial was over, some of the jurors made statements for the television program which revealed that they were not capable of judging the case. Yet Christians will trust that crowd rather than take their cases to other believers who do have spiritual discernment.

> **I speak to your shame. Is it so, that there is not a wise man among you? no, not one that shall be able to judge between his brethren?**
>
> **But brother goeth to law with brother, and that before the unbelievers [1 Cor. 6:5–6].**

Of course, not every Christian is a capable judge, but Paul is saying, "I speak to your shame, isn't there a wise man among you?" When you go to a secular court, you are saying that none of the saints are capable of judging. Well, I know some dear brethren in the Lord with whom I would be willing to risk my life. I am confident they would render a just verdict.

Now why does a Christian have a capability to judge? Paul will give us three reasons:

> **And such were some of you: but ye are washed, but ye are sanctified, but ye are justified in the name of the Lord Jesus, and by the Spirit of our God [1 Cor. 6:11].**

"Ye are washed." It is "not by works of righteousness which we have done, but according to his mercy he saved us, by the washing of regeneration . . ." (Titus 3:5). We have been born again, washed. Because the mercy of God has reached down and touched us, we ought to know how to extend mercy. We can be merciful because we have experienced mercy. We should recognize that there are many wonderful believers today who have been washed. We should trust ourselves to them rather than to the unsaved.

"Ye are sanctified." Sanctification in the Corinthian epistles is of two kinds, but I think here it means positional sanctification, that is, being *in* Christ. This means that Christ is on our side and all believers are brothers in Christ. If another Christian judges me, it means that one of my *brothers* is judging me. I would be willing to trust myself to the judgment of a brother. A little girl was carrying a heavy baby down the street. A man saw her and asked, "Little girl, isn't that baby too heavy for you?" "Oh, no," she said, "he's my *brother*." The relationship makes a lot of difference. A brother is not too heavy. I am in Christ and my brother is in Christ; so I should be willing to trust my brother.

"Ye are justified." The third reason my brother is capable of being a judge is that his sins are already forgiven, as mine are. He has been declared righteous before the throne of God, as I have been. "Who shall lay any thing to the charge of God's elect? It is God that justifieth" (Rom. 8:33). "But to him that worketh not, but believeth on him that justifieth the ungodly, his faith is counted for righteousness" (Rom. 4:5). A fellow Christian knows this, and I feel that he could handle my case better than anyone else.

THE BELIEVER'S BODY IS THE TEMPLE
OF THE HOLY SPIRIT

All things are lawful unto me, but all things are not expedient: all things are lawful for me, but I will not be brought under the power of any [1 Cor. 6:12].

There are a lot of things which a believer can do, but they are not expedient to do. I could mention many things; Paul mentions one here:

Meats for the belly, and the belly for meats: but God shall destroy both it and them. Now the body is not for fornication, but for the Lord; and the Lord for the body [1 Cor. 6:13].

Meats shall be destroyed someday. Our stomachs shall be destroyed someday. There is Christian liberty in what we eat.

In contrast, our bodies are not to be used for fornication. Our bodies belong to the Lord.

And God hath both raised up the Lord, and will also raise up us by his own power.

Know ye not that your bodies are the members of Christ? shall I then take the members of Christ, and make them the members of an harlot? God forbid [1 Cor. 6:14–15].

Young folk today think that they can live together without being married. One such couple came to me wanting to talk about getting into Christian service. They weren't married, but they were living together! I told them, "You get married." They asked, "Why?" I said, "Because God commands it. That is the way God wants it to be. Until you are willing to do that, you cannot serve Him."

What? know ye not that he which is joined to an harlot is one body? for two, saith he, shall be one flesh.

But he that is joined unto the Lord is one spirit.

Flee fornication. Every sin that a man doeth is without the body; but he that committeth fornication sinneth against his own body [1 Cor. 6:16–18].

My friend, you cannot live in immorality and serve Christ. Unfortunately, we find that public opinion generally accepts immoral persons; but God does not accept them.

What? know ye not that your body is the temple of the Holy Ghost which is in you, which ye have of God, and ye are not your own?

For ye are bought with a price: therefore glorify God in your body, and in your spirit, which are God's [1 Cor. 6:19–20].

Here is a remarkable truth which many believers have not received. Our bodies are the temple of the Holy Spirit. Because our bodies belong to God, we are not to share our bodies in fornication. This leads to a discussion of marriage, which will be the subject of the next chapter.

CHAPTER 7

THEME: Marriage

This chapter concerns marriage; so we shall be discussing the subject of sex. I think we will probably handle it in a more dignified manner than is usual today because we are going to follow Paul.

In the previous chapter Paul had given them the spiritual truths that, by application to the problem of marriage, can solve matters that relate to sex in marriage. You will remember that he emphasized that our bodies belong to God and that our bodies are the temple of the Holy Ghost. Our bodies are to be used for the glory of God.

Now concerning the things whereof ye wrote unto me: It is good for a man not to touch a woman [1 Cor. 7:1].

It is obvious that the Corinthian believers had written a letter to Paul concerning this problem. We do not have the question, but we do have Paul's answer. Paul has taken a long time to get to this. He first dealt with the divisions and the scandals in their midst. However, he has no reluctance in dealing with the subject of marriage, and he writes boldly and very frankly. Before we get into the text itself, I wish to deal with two introductory matters.

First there is the question: Was Paul ever married? If Paul was never married, then in his explanation he is simply theorizing. He is not speaking from experience. However, Paul did not do that. Paul always spoke from experience. It was not the method of the Spirit of God to choose a man who knew nothing about the subject on which the Spirit of God wanted him to write.

It has always been assumed that Paul was not married on the basis of the seventh verse: "For I would that all men were even as I myself. But every man hath his proper gift of God, one after this manner, and another after that." If we are going to assume that Paul was not married, we need to pay attention to the verse that follows: "I say therefore to the unmarried and widows, It is good for them if they abide even as I." Someone will say, "He still says that he is unmarried." Granted. We know he was not married. But notice that he mentions two classes here: the unmarried and the widows (or widowers). He could have been unmarried or a widower.

It is difficult to believe that Paul had always been unmarried because of his background and because of who he was. Paul was a member of the Sanhedrin. In Acts 26:10 Paul says, "Which thing I also did in Jerusalem: and many of the saints did I shut up in prison, having received authority from the chief priests; and when they were put to death, I gave my voice against them." How could he give his *voice* against them? It was by his vote in the Sanhedrin, which means he was a member of the Sanhedrin. Since Paul was a member of the Sanhedrin, he must have been a married man because that was one of the conditions of membership.

There was an insistence upon Jewish young men to marry. The Mishna said this should be at the age of eighteen. In the *Yebhamoth*, in the commentary on Genesis 5:2 it states: "A Jew who has no wife is not a man." I believe it is an inescapable conclusion that Paul at one time was a married man. He undoubtedly was a widower who had never remarried. In chapter 9 we read, "Have we not power to lead about a sister, a wife, as well as other apostles, and as the brethren of the Lord, and Cephas?" (1 Cor 9:5). I think Paul is saying, "I could marry again if I wanted to; I would be permitted to do that. But I'm not going to for the simple reason that I would not ask a woman to follow me around in the type of ministry God has given to me."

It is my conviction that in the past Paul had loved some good woman who had reciprocated his love because he spoke so tenderly of the marriage relationship. "Husbands, love your wives, even as Christ also loved the church, and gave himself for it" (Eph. 5:25).

I would like to give you a quotation from F. W. Farrar who writes in his *Life and Work of St. Paul:* "The other question which arises is, Was Saul married? Had he the support of some loving heart during the fiery struggles of his youth? Amid the to-and-fro contentions of spirit which resulted from an imperfect and unsatisfying creed, was there in the troubled sea of his life one little island home where he could find refuge from incessant thoughts? Little as we know of his domestic relations, little as he cared to mingle mere private interests with the great spiritual truths which occupy his soul, it seems to me that we must answer this question in the affirmative."

The position of many expositors is that Paul had been married and that his wife had died. Paul never made reference to her, but because he spoke so tenderly of the marriage relationship, I believe he had been married.

The second introductory matter is not a question but a statement. We need to understand the Corinth of that day. If we do not, we are going to fall into the trap of saying that Paul is commending the single state above the married state. One must understand the local situation of Corinth to know what he is talking about. Notice the first two verses again.

> Now concerning the things whereof ye wrote unto me: It is good for a man not to touch a woman.
>
> Nevertheless, to avoid fornication, let every man have his own wife, and let every woman have her own husband [1 Cor. 7:1–2].

We need to understand Corinth. I have been to the ruins of ancient Corinth. Towering above those ruins is the mountain which was the acropolis, called Acro-Corinthus. The city was dominated by the Acro-Corinthus, and on top of it was the temple of Aphrodite. It towered over the city like a dark cloud. Today the ruins of a Crusader fort are there. When the Crusaders came, they used the stones from the temple of Aphrodite to build their fortress.

This temple was like most heathen temples. Sex was a religion. There were one thousand so-called vestal virgins there. In that temple you could get food, drink, and sex. Those vestal virgins were nothing in the world but one thousand prostitutes. Sex was carried on in the name of religion. That was the philosophy of Plato, by the way.

People tend to forget the immorality of that culture. A man once said to me, "Socrates wrote in a very lofty language." Yes, sometimes he did. He also told prostitutes how they ought to conduct themselves. The whole thought was to get rid of the desires of the body by satisfying them. That is heathenism. That came out in two basic philosophies of the Greeks. Stoicism said the basic desires were to be denied; Epicureanism said they were to be fulfilled all the way.

The wife in the Roman world was a chattel. She was a workhorse. A man generally had several wives. One had charge of the kitchen, another had charge of the living area, another was in charge of the clothes. Sex was secondary because the man went up to the temple where the good-looking girls were kept. There they celebrated the seasons of fertility, and believe me, friend, that is what was carried on.

You will still find the same thing among the Bedouins in Palestine today. They have several wives, and it is a practical thing for them. One takes care of the sheep, another goes with the man as he wanders around, another stays back at the home base where they have a tent and probably a few fruit trees. He thinks he needs at least three wives.

Now Paul lifts marriage up to the heights, out of this degradation, and says to the Corinthians they are not to live like that. Every man is to have one wife, and every woman is to have her own husband. Paul lifted woman from the place of slavery in the pagan world, the Roman Empire, and made her a companion of man. He restored her to her rightful position. He was in Ephesus when he wrote to the Corinthians, and in Ephesus there was much the same thing in the awful temple of Diana. It was to the Ephesians that Paul wrote, "Husbands, love your wives, even as Christ also loved the church, and gave himself for it" (Eph. 5:25).

Now I know somebody is going to say that he also told wives to obey their husbands. I would like to know where he said that. He did write, "Wives, submit yourselves unto your own husbands, as unto the Lord" (Eph. 5:22). Have you ever looked up the word *submit* to see what it means? To submit means to respond. Wives are to respond to their own husbands. The wife is to react to the man. Man is the aggressor. He initiates the expression of love, and the woman is the receiver. This is not a matter of sex alone; it involves a couple mentally, spiritually, psychologically, and physically. Man is the aggressor; woman is the receiver.

God created man and woman that way in the beginning. He created woman as the "helpmeet," a helper suitable for him or corresponding to him. She is the other part of man. When a husband says, "I love you," she answers, "I love you." When a man admits that he has a cold wife, he is really saying that he is a failure as a husband and that he is to blame for the condition.

Paul lifts woman from the slave state to that of a partner of man. Listen to the next verse:

Let the husband render unto the wife due benevolence: and likewise also the wife unto the husband [1 Cor. 7:3].

She is to respond to him. He is to tell her that he loves her.

The wife hath not power of her own body, but the husband: and likewise also the husband hath not power of his own body, but the wife [1 Cor. 7:4].

The man is not to run up to that temple of Aphrodite. That is sin. Love and sex are to take place at home. That is exactly what he is saying here. The only motive for marriage is love—not sex, but love. I am convinced that Paul had known the love of a good and great woman.

So many of the great men in Scripture knew the love of a woman. There are Adam and Eve, Jacob and Rachel, Boaz and Ruth, David and Abigail—it was Abigail who told David, ". . . the soul of my lord shall be bound in the bundle of life with the LORD thy God . . ." (1 Sam. 25:29).

It is said of John Wesley that when he came to America he was not a saved man. He wrote, "I came to this country to convert Indians, but who is going to convert John Wesley?" The story goes that the crown had sent to America an insipid nobleman. Due to the terrible custom of that day, the nobility was entitled to marry the finest, and he had married a woman of striking beauty and strong personality, who also was an outstanding Christian. Then there came into their colony this fiery young missionary. And these two fell in love. But she said, "No, John, God has called you to go back to England to do some great ser-

vice for Him." It was she who sent John Wesley back to England—to
marry the Methodist Church. Back in England Wesley was converted,
and she was his inspiration. Behind every great man is a great
woman.

Now Paul continues his guidelines for conduct in marriage.

> **Defraud ye not one the other, except it be with consent
> for a time, that ye may give yourselves to fasting and
> prayer; and come together again, that Satan tempt you
> not for your incontinency.**
>
> **But I speak this by permission, and not of command-
> ment [1 Cor. 7:5–6].**

He says this is not a commandment, but it is a guideline to follow so
that Satan will not have an opportunity to tempt either member of the
marriage relationship.

> **For I would that all men were even as I myself. But every
> man hath his proper gift of God, one after this manner,
> and another after that [1 Cor. 7:7].**

At this time Paul did not have a wife. He did not remarry. He was not
taking a wife along with him on his travels.

There are people in the Lord's work who have not married. They
have made that kind of sacrifice—some for several years, some for
their whole lifetime. You remember that the Lord Jesus said, "For
there are some eunuchs, which were so born from their mother's
womb: and there are some eunuchs, which were made eunuchs of
men: and there be eunuchs, which have made themselves eunuchs for
the kingdom of heaven's sake . . ." (Matt. 19:12).

When I began in the ministry, I attempted to imitate a man who
was a bachelor. I thought that was the happiest state, but I soon
learned that it wasn't for me. I wanted a wife. Paul says that is all
right—"every man hath his proper gift of God."

> I say therefore to the unmarried and widows, It is good
> for them if they abide even as I.

> But if they cannot contain, let them marry: for it is better
> to marry than to burn [1 Cor. 7:8-9].

It is better to marry than to burn with passion.

COMMAND TO THE MARRIED

> And unto the married I command, yet not I, but the
> Lord, Let not the wife depart from her husband:

> But and if she depart, let her remain unmarried, or be
> reconciled to her husband: and let not the husband put
> away his wife [1 Cor. 7:10-11].

Here is a commandment. Paul is putting it on the line. The wife is
not to leave her husband, and the husband is not to leave his wife. If
one or the other is going to leave, then they are to remain unmarried.
Now there was a new problem which presented itself in Corinth.
After Paul had come and had preached the gospel to them, a husband
in a family would accept Christ but the wife would not. In another
family it might be that the wife would accept Christ and the husband
would not. What were the believers to do under such circumstances?

> But to the rest speak I, not the Lord: If any brother hath
> a wife that believeth not, and she be pleased to dwell
> with him, let him not put her away.

> And the woman which hath an husband that believeth
> not, and if he be pleased to dwell with her, let her not
> leave him.

> For the unbelieving husband is sanctified by the wife,
> and the unbelieving wife is sanctified by the husband:
> else were your children unclean; but now are they holy
> [1 Cor. 7:12-14].

If one was married to an unsaved man or to an unsaved woman and there were children in the family, Paul said they should try to see it through. Paul says, "Stay right where you are if you can."

> But if the unbelieving depart, let him depart. A brother
> or a sister is not under bondage in such cases: but God
> hath called us to peace [1 Cor. 7:15].

If the unbeliever walks out of the marriage, that is another story. Then the believer is free. Now the question which is asked is whether that one is free to marry again. I believe that under certain circumstances Paul would have given permission for that. I do not think one can put down a categorical rule either way for today. I think that each case stands or falls on its own merits. I'm afraid this can easily be abused, even by Christians. I am afraid sometimes a husband or a wife tries to get rid of the other and forces them to leave in order that they might have a "scriptural ground" for divorce.

> For what knowest thou, O wife, whether thou shalt save
> thy husband? or how knowest thou, O man, whether
> thou shalt save thy wife? [1 Cor. 7:16].

This should be the goal of the wife. I know several women who were married to unsaved men and tried to win them for Christ. This also should be the goal of the husband who is married to an unsaved woman. Winning them for Christ should be uppermost in their consideration.

> But as God hath distributed to every man, as the Lord
> hath called every one, so let him walk. And so ordain I
> in all churches [1 Cor. 7:17].

Paul is advising people to stay in the situation in which they are. They are not to walk out of their marriage after they have heard and accepted the gospel. They are to stay married if the unbelieving partner will allow it.

This ought to answer the question for today. Unfortunately, there are some ministers and evangelists who have advised people who have had a divorce and have remarried to go back to their first mate after they had come to Christ. May I say, I can't think of anything more tragic than that kind of advice. I know one woman who finally ended up in a mental institution because she followed the advice of some evangelist who told her to leave her second husband and her lovely Christian home and go back to a drunken husband whom she had previously divorced. How foolish can one be? We need to understand what Paul is saying here.

> **Is any man called being circumcised? let him not become uncircumcised. Is any called in uncircumcision? let him not be circumcised.**
>
> **Circumcision is nothing, and uncircumcision is nothing, but the keeping of the commandments of God.**
>
> **Let every man abide in the same calling wherein he was called [1 Cor. 7:18–20].**

Paul now expands the application of this principle. It applies to other relationships in life. For instance, if when you are converted you belong to the circumcised, that is, if you are an Israelite, don't try to become a Gentile. If you are a Gentile, don't try to become an Israelite. Circumcision or uncircumcision is no longer important. Obedience to Christ is the issue now. The Israelite and the Gentile are one in Christ.

The whole point here is that in whatever state you find yourself when you accept Christ, stay right there. I have known many businessmen who get into some Christian organization after their conversion, and the next thing I know they come to me and say that they are thinking of giving up the business and going into full-time Christian work. My friend, if you are a successful businessman, God may have given you a gift to minister in that particular area. He may not intend for you to change and go into full-time Christian work. Let's go on and listen to what Paul says.

Art thou called being a servant? care not for it: but if thou mayest be made free, use it rather.

For he that is called in the Lord, being a servant, is the Lord's freeman: likewise also he that is called, being free, is Christ's servant [1 Cor. 7:21-22].

In that day there were slaves and freemen. If a person were a slave or a servant of a man, he was not to try to get loosed from that, thinking that God wanted him to be freed from his master.

I find today that there are many housewives who get the notion that they are to become great Bible teachers. They get so involved in it that they neglect their families.

I shall never forget the story I heard about the late Gypsy Smith. A woman came to him in Dallas, Texas, and said, "Gypsy Smith, I feel called to go into the ministry." He asked her a very pertinent question (he had a way of doing that), "Are you married?" She said that she was. "How many children do you have?" She answered that she had five. He said, "That's wonderful. God has called you into the ministry, and He has already given you your congregation!"

Ye are bought with a price; be not ye the servants of men [1 Cor. 7:23].

You have been redeemed by the blood of Jesus Christ. Now don't be a slave to someone. Does this sound like a contradiction? Let me explain by an example. A cocktail waitress was converted by hearing the gospel on our radio broadcast. Everything about the Bible was brand new to her. She asked me a question about whether she should give up being a cocktail waitress because she just didn't feel right about it. I answered her that it was up to her. I said, "That is a decision that you must make. If you have a conviction about it, then give it up. If you want to know what I think about it personally, I think you ought to give it up. However don't give it up because I say so, but give it up if that becomes your conviction." She did give it up and found another job within a couple of weeks. She had been bought with a price; she was not to be a servant of man.

Brethren, let every man, wherein he is called, therein abide with God [1 Cor. 7:24].

This is the important consideration. When a person is converted, whatever he is doing, wherever he is, he is to remain in that position as long as he is free in his relationship to God. God must be first. "Therein abide with God." If his situation will not permit God to be first, then he should change the situation, as the cocktail waitress did.

CONCERNING MARRIAGEABLE DAUGHTERS

The discussion for the remainder of this chapter is an answer to the second question which the Corinthians had asked Paul and is related to the first question. Remember that all this must be interpreted in the light of what Corinth was in Paul's day, and then it can be applied to the day in which we live. Corinth was such a corrupt place, and manhood was corrupted there. When womanhood is corrupted, manhood will descend to a low level—that has always been the story. So there was this question among Christian parents in Corinth: What should they do about their marriageable daughters? Before they were converted, their friends were drunken sots who went up to the temple of Aphrodite to the prostitutes there. What should the single Christian girls do now? Paul will deal with this question.

Now concerning virgins I have no commandment of the Lord: yet I give my judgment, as one that hath obtained mercy of the Lord to be faithful [1 Cor. 7:25].

"Now concerning virgins"—several of the translations have it: "Now concerning virgin *daughters*," which I think clarifies it. That is really what he is talking about here.

This reveals that Paul knew the commandments of the Lord Jesus Christ and what He taught. However, he specifically says here that concerning virgins he has no commandment of the Lord. "But," he says, "I give my own judgment." He is giving his opinion as a capable judge because he had obtained the mercy of God and he wanted to be

faithful to God. In other words, he possessed the qualifications a
judge should have as he had told them in chapter 6.

> **I suppose therefore that this is good for the present dis-
> tress, I say, that it is good for a man so to be.**

> **Art thou bound unto a wife? seek not to be loosed. Art
> thou loosed from a wife? seek not a wife [1 Cor.
> 7:26–27].**

"The present distress" was that awful situation in Corinth which Paul
knew was not going to continue. Someone asked me, "Do you think
this excessive immorality and this lawlessness in our nation will continue?" If it does continue, my friend, it will bring down our houses
and destroy our nation—then it will be ended for sure.

Now what does he say? In the present distress, since you have
come to Christ at such a difficult time, if you are bound to a wife, stay
with her. If she is unsaved, stay with her as long as you can. If you are
not married, then, because of the present distress with the tremendous immorality that is here, it would be best for you to remain single.
Paul says this is his judgment.

> **But and if thou marry, thou hast not sinned; and if a
> virgin marry, she hath not sinned. Nevertheless such
> shall have trouble in the flesh: but I spare you [1 Cor.
> 7:28].**

Of course it is not sinful to marry. But the sea of matrimony is rough
under the most favorable circumstances. He is trying to save them
from much trouble. That reminds me of the country boy who was being married. The preacher said to him, "Wilt thou have this woman to
be thy lawfully wedded wife?" The young fellow answered, "I wilt."
And I guess he did! In our day we are seeing the shipwreck of a growing number of marriages—even among Christians. The divorces in
Southern California are now about equal in number to the marriages.
That reveals we also have a "present distress."

Now Paul goes on to discuss other things with them, all in the light of the present distress, the shortness of time, the urgency and immediacy of the hour. He mentions five things which are necessary, which are inevitable, and which are the common experience of mankind in this world. He discusses marriage, sorrow, joy, commerce, and then relation to the world in general.

Marriage is the first one he discusses. "Sure," Paul says in effect, "It is all right to go ahead and marry, but remember that you will have trouble." And they will. In counseling I have tried to tell young people that the romantic period will pass. When the first month's rent comes due and there is not much money in the treasury, believe me, romance flies out the window.

> **But this I say, brethren, the time is short: it remaineth, that both they that have wives be as though they had none [1 Cor. 7:29].**

Paul is saying that in spite of the stress of the times, they are to put God first. If you are married, can you act as if you are not married in that you put God first?

> **And they that weep, as though they wept not; and they that rejoice, as though they rejoiced not; and they that buy, as though they possessed not [1 Cor. 7:30].**

"And they that weep, as though they wept not." Are you going to let some sorrow, some tragedy in your life keep you from serving God?

"And they that rejoice, as though they rejoiced not." Are you going to let pleasure take the place of your relationship to God, as many do?

"And they that buy, as though they possessed not." Will you let your business take the place of God? Many a man has made business his god.

> **And they that use this world, as not abusing it: for the fashion of this world passeth away [1 Cor. 7:31].**

You and I are in the world, not *of* the world; but this doesn't mean that we are to walk around with an attitude of touch not, taste not, handle not. We are to use this world. This past summer I made a trip up into the Northwest, and I stopped many times to look upon those glorious forests that they have up there. I used them—they blessed my heart. I enjoyed them. But I didn't fall down and worship any one of those trees! We are to use the things of this world but not abuse them. We are not to substitute them for the Creator.

"The fashion of this world passeth away." Do the things of this life control your life, or does Christ control your life? This is what Paul is talking about.

Now he goes back to a discussion of marriage.

But I would have you without carefulness. He that is unmarried careth for the things that belong to the Lord, how he may please the Lord [1 Cor. 7:32].

Paul now gives some practical observations. The unmarried person doesn't have to worry about changing the baby's diapers or going out to buy food for the family. He or she can give his or her time to the things of God.

But he that is married careth for the things that are of the world, how he may please his wife [1 Cor. 7:33].

The married man tries to please his wife. This is normal and natural, and Paul is not saying it is wrong.

There is difference also between a wife and a virgin. The unmarried woman careth for the things of the Lord, that she may be holy both in body and in spirit: but she that is married careth for the things of the world, how she may please her husband.

And this I speak for your own profit; not that I may cast a snare upon you, but for that which is comely, and that

ye may attend upon the Lord without distraction [1 Cor. 7:34-35].

Paul is making it very clear that the important thing is to put God first. That should be the determining factor for every person in a marriage relationship. I don't care who you are or how spiritual you think you may be, if you are not putting God first in your marriage, then your marriage, my friend, is not the ideal Christian marriage.

He comes back to his judgment that the single person can attend upon the Lord without distraction.

The wife is bound by the law as long as her husband liveth; but if her husband be dead, she is at liberty to be married to whom she will; only in the Lord [1 Cor. 7:39].

That is, she is to marry another Christian, of course.

But she is happier if she so abide, after my judgment: and I think also that I have the Spirit of God [1 Cor. 7:40].

Paul makes it clear again that this is his judgment, his advice. The important thing is to serve God, to put God first in your life. If a person is married, God should still be first in his life. Unfortunately, there are many Christian couples who are compatible—they are not going to the divorce court—but God does not have first place in their marriage.

In deciding your marital status, the most important consideration is not what your Christian friends will say or how society in general will regard you. The question you need to ask yourself is: In what way can I put God first in my life?

CHAPTER 8

THEME: Christian liberty regarding eating meat

We are in the section of the epistle dealing with Christian liberty, which extends from chapter 8 to the first verse of chapter 11. It touches on several aspects of Christian liberty. Chapter 8 deals with the problem of whether or not we should eat meat and the liberty that a child of God should have in this particular area.

We need to recognize as we go through this section of the epistle that Paul is writing to the Corinthians and that he has called them carnal, babes in Christ. He deals first with carnalities, and later he will deal with spiritualities. Since it is in the level of carnalities that the contemporary church lives and moves and has its being, this section is pertinent for you and me.

The subject of diet is just as controversial as marriage and divorce. Diet is a fad with many people. (Right at the moment diet is more than a fad with me because my doctor has put me on a very strict diet.)

Diet generally is an essential part of the ritual of many of the cults and "isms." Many of them have stringent rules about diet. It is interesting that God in the Old Testament gave Israel certain restrictions about eating meat. An edible animal had a parted hoof and chewed the cud. That eliminated the pig whose hoof is parted but does not chew the cud. There were also certain fowl and fish which were designated by name as unfit for food. You can find these listed in the Book of Leviticus and also in Deuteronomy, chapter 14.

A friend of mine, who belonged to a cult that would not eat pork, was discussing this with me one day. So I asked him, "Have you ever eaten ossifrage?" "A what?" "An ossifrage." "Well," he said, "I don't even know what it is." So I told him, "You'd better find out what it is because you may come to my house someday and I might serve you roast ossifrage, which for you would be as wrong to eat as pork." It is amazing that the cults that place such importance on the Old Testament dietary regulations are so ignorant of the actual details.

Why did God give a special diet to Israel? He makes it very clear: "Ye are the children of the LORD your God: ye shall not cut yourselves, nor make any baldness between your eyes for the dead. For thou art an holy people unto the LORD thy God, and the LORD hath chosen thee to be a peculiar people unto himself, above all the nations that are upon the earth. Thou shalt not eat any abominable thing" (Deut. 14:1–3). Also, I do believe that diet is important for health. God gave Israel foods that were good for them. Even doctors today prescribe diets which exclude certain foods.

The Bible puts up a red light and is very specific on many things which are wrong for us to do. For example, God condemns drunkenness. There can be no argument nor question about that. However, there is a gray area, questionable practices, doubtful things about which the Bible is silent. These are things which are neither black nor white, and the Bible doesn't give us specific instructions. For example: Should a Christian smoke? In the South they think that mixed bathing is wrong and smoking is all right. On the West Coast boys and girls, men and women swim together without compunction, but they condemn smoking. There are different rules which have been put down by certain groups of Christians. They may be good rules or they may be bad rules—I'm not going to argue about that. What I want you to see is the great principle which Paul is laying down here.

There is another preliminary consideration which is an understanding of Corinth in Paul's day. If you do not understand the background, you will miss the whole point of the chapter. It is this: the best place to eat in Corinth was not at the swankiest restaurant; the best place to get good meat was in the meat shop that was run by the temple.

In Corinth the people brought sacrifices of animals to offer to the idols. They would bring the best animals they had. The meat was offered to the idol, but it didn't stay there long because they believed that the spirit of the idol ate the spirit of the animal—and that finished the meal for the idol. Then they took the meat to the shambles or stalls around the temple, which was the meat market where the meat was sold. If you wanted to buy filet or the best steaks or the best prime rib roast in Corinth, you had to go to one of those shops at the temple to get meat which had been offered to idols.

Some of the Christians in Corinth were offended by this practice and were asking Paul about it. They would be invited out to dinner with another Christian family and would be served a lovely filet mignon. During the course of the conversation they would say, "My, this is wonderful meat. Where did you get it?" The lady would answer that she got it at the temple meat market. This would offend the couple who felt that it was wrong to eat anything that had been offered to idols. This is the question which Paul discusses in this chapter. Should a Christian eat meat that had been offered to idols? This was a real problem to the people in Corinth because many of them had come out of that background of idolatry, and they thought it was a compromise with idolatry. Others in the church felt that it made no difference. Let's listen to Paul as he discusses this problem in the city of Corinth.

CHRISTIAN LIBERTY CONCERNING MEAT

Now as touching things offered unto idols, we know that we all have knowledge. Knowledge puffeth up, but charity edifieth.

And if any man think that he knoweth any thing, he knoweth nothing yet as he ought to know [1 Cor. 8:1-2].

Knowledge blows up like a balloon or like an automobile tire. Love doesn't blow up, but it fills up. Love for God and love for others should determine our conduct. Knowledge alone puffs up and tends to make us harsh in our dealings with others. This is a danger with a great many folk who feel that they have a lot of knowledge and yet in reality know very little.

Let me give an illustration. We had just concluded a service at a Bible conference in which six young men had received Christ. A man came to me and insisted that I break away from everyone else and discuss with him the subject of election (he erroneously felt that I had alluded to it in my message). I took a few moments to talk with him until I discovered that he didn't want to discuss it; he wanted to tell me what he thought about election. I discovered that he had been reading on that subject recently and that he thought he knew everything about it. As I listened to him, I could picture myself as a young seminary student going into the office of a theological professor to tell him what I thought about election. I thought I was telling him something he didn't know! Well, I don't care what stage of spiritual development you are in today, you don't know everything about any subject—and I don't either. All of us are in the learning process. Paul could say of himself, "That I may know him, and the power of his resurrection, and the fellowship of his sufferings . . ." (Phil. 3:10). It is the knowledge of Christ which we need above everything else. If the man who wanted to argue about election had been governed by love, he would have been rejoicing over the conversion of these young men and would not have taken me away from folk who needed encouragement and counsel.

Paul is saying that we have a certain knowledge and, because of that certain knowledge, our behavior is governed by it.

But if any man love God, the same is known of him [1 Cor. 8:3].

We ought to be governed by love rather than knowledge.

As concerning therefore the eating of those things that are offered in sacrifice unto idols, we know that an idol is nothing in the world, and that there is none other God but one [1 Cor. 8:4].

After you have come to Christ, after you have the Word of God, you know that an idol is nothing. That is the way Paul spoke of the idols—they are nothing. There is but one God. So he says that the meat that was offered to the idol was not affected. Nothing happened to it. It was not contaminated. In fact, it was prime meat. So the instructed Christian could go there to get his meat and eat it with no problem.

> For though there be that are called gods, whether in
> heaven or in earth, (as there be gods many, and lords
> many,)
>
> But to us there is but one God, the Father, of whom are
> all things, and we in him; and one Lord Jesus Christ, by
> whom are all things, and we by him [1 Cor. 8:5-6].

These idols were merely called gods. As I stood in the ruins of the
temple of Apollo in Corinth, I thought of this passage of Scripture.
I thought of all the sacrifices that had been offered to that image of
Apollo there. It was nothing. The meat was brought in to the idol, put
there for a little while, and then it was taken to the meat shop. It didn't
make any difference in the meat—the idol was nothing. The instructed Christian knew that. He knew there is but one God, the
Father, and that there is but one Lord Jesus Christ. He made all things,
and all things belong to Him.

> Howbeit there is not in every man that knowledge: for
> some with conscience of the idol unto this hour eat it as a
> thing offered unto an idol; and their conscience being
> weak is defiled [1 Cor. 8:7].

The weak ones, the babes in Christ, the carnal Christians, these were
the ones who were offended by the meat offered to idols. They did not
have the knowledge. Their consciences bothered them. So they criti-
cized the others who felt at liberty to eat the meat.

May I say that we still find the same thing today. We have people
who call themselves separated Christians. They think they are being
very spiritual when, actually, they are revealing that they don't have
the knowledge. They are the ones who say you can't do this and that.
They are the ones who are offended at Christians who use their Christian liberty. They are like the Christians at Corinth who were offended
when they were served meat offered to idols and said, "Oh, no, we are
separated. We won't touch that meat." That kind of separation is not
due to spirituality; it is due to ignorance.

Now Paul lays down a great principle:

But meat commendeth us not to God: for neither, if we eat, are we the better; neither, if we eat not, are we the worse [1 Cor. 8:8].

Meat has nothing to do with our relationship to God.

You will remember that Simon Peter had trouble with this. He had been brought up to consider certain things unclean according to the Mosaic Law. When the sheet came down from heaven in his vision and the Lord told Peter to arise and eat, Peter refused. He said, ". . . Not so, Lord; for I have never eaten any thing that is common or unclean" (Acts 10:14). (He calls Him Lord at the same time that he is failing to obey Him.) Then the Lord said, ". . . What God hath cleansed, that call not thou common" (Acts 10:15). In other words, God is no longer making the distinction between the clean and the unclean animals. That is passed. Now we can eat any animal that we wish to eat.

Down in San Antonio, Texas, they can rattlesnake meat. Now if you are going to have rattlesnake for dinner, please don't invite me to come over. This has nothing to do with religious scruples, but it has a lot to do with a weak stomach.

Paul has stated a great principle here. Meat does not commend you to God. You may do as you please in such matters. This is the liberty that a believer has.

But take heed lest by any means this liberty of yours become a stumblingblock to them that are weak [1 Cor. 8:9].

Now it is not a question of it being right or wrong to eat meat. It is a concern for others. You have the liberty to eat the meat if you want to. But what about your concern for others? You have the knowledge, but what about your love? Do you have love for your weak brother? Are you concerned how this will affect him?

For if any man see thee which hast knowledge sit at meat in the idol's temple, shall not the conscience of him which is weak be emboldened to eat those things which are offered to idols [1 Cor. 8:10].

The reason many of us who are in Christian service do not do certain things is so that we may not offend others. Let me give an illustration. There was a time when I loved to dance. In fact, I was chairman of the dance committee of an organization before I accepted Christ. After I started studying for the ministry, I gave up dancing.

In college the president of the ministerial students was also president of the student body, and he was active in promoting dancing. Knowing I had been chairman of a dance committee, he tried to get me to help him. I told him, "No. I can't do that." I am not going to argue if it was right or wrong because it is not a question of knowledge. There are many things I am at liberty to do which I do not do. Why? Well, my decision is on the basis of love. I do not want to hurt my weak brother. Because of my example, he might be out there on the floor dancing the fandango—or whatever they dance today—and I don't want to be responsible for drawing him away from the Lord. He is a weak brother.

> **And through thy knowledge shall the weak brother perish, for whom Christ died? [1 Cor. 8:11].**

You see, we operate on a different principle. It is not a question of an activity being right or wrong. It is a question of its effect on that weak brother or upon your neighbor. You see, knowledge, after all is a very dangerous thing.

> **But when ye sin so against the brethren, and wound their weak conscience, ye sin against Christ [1 Cor. 8:12].**

When we are responsible for a believer falling away from Christ, we are affecting Christ Himself.

> **Wherefore, if meat make my brother to offend, I will eat no flesh while the world standeth, lest I make my brother to offend [1 Cor. 8:13].**

Here is the motivation for action on these things. Paul will go over this same principle again in chapter 10, "All things are lawful for me, but all things are not expedient: all things are lawful for me, but all things edify not" (1 Cor. 10:23).

There is no point in arguing about whether something is right or wrong. It is a question of the effect upon the weak brother. It is not a question of knowledge. All things are lawful for me. The liberty of the Christian is not pinned down by legality. He is not circumscribed by rules of conduct. His liberty is limited by love. His motivation should be not to offend the brother but to be a blessing to him. That is how to determine Christian conduct. That is the motivation for Christian conduct. My knowledge can tell me that it is perfectly all right for me to do something, but my love for the weak brother will keep me from doing it.

CHAPTER 9

THEME: Christian liberty regarding service for Christ

In chapter 8 Paul dealt with the matter of Christian liberty in regard to eating meat which had been offered to idols. The principle he laid down was that in doubtful matters the motive for Christian conduct was regard for fellow believers. We won't do anything which causes a weak brother to stumble.

This shows us that there is a limitation on our Christian liberty. This can be stated in a graphic way. You have a perfect right to swing your fist any way you want to, but where my nose begins your liberty ends.

Paul lays down this principle several times in the Epistle to the Corinthians. "All things are lawful unto me, but all things are not expedient: all things are lawful for me, but I will not be brought under the power of any" (1 Cor. 6:12). "But meat commendeth us not to God: for neither, if we eat, are we the better; neither, if we eat not, are we the worse" (1 Cor. 8:8). "All things are lawful for me, but all things are not expedient: all things are lawful for me, but all things edify not" (1 Cor. 10:23). He goes on to say that no man should seek his own, but every man should seek the good of his neighbor. Christian liberty has its limitations for this reason.

Now Paul is going to illustrate this matter of Christian liberty in another field. He will discuss his own right as an apostle, his official right. Then he will discuss his right to be supported by the church. He had the right to expect the church to care for him and all his needs as a preacher of the gospel. He uses these personal matters to illustrate Christian liberty.

Paul first defends his official right as an apostle. Paul was in the habit of defending his apostleship because it was challenged in many places.

Am I not an apostle? am I not free? have I not seen Jesus

Christ our Lord? are not ye my work in the Lord? [1 Cor. 9:1].

"Am I not an apostle?" Of course the answer is, "Yes, Paul, you are an apostle." The way this question is couched in the Greek demands a positive answer.

"Am I not free?" The answer is, "Yes, Paul, you are free."

"Have I not seen Jesus Christ our Lord?" One qualification of an apostle was that he had personally seen Jesus Christ. Paul had satisfied that requirement.

"Are not ye my work in the Lord?" The Corinthian believers were the evidence of his apostleship.

If I be not an apsotle unto others, yet doubtless I am to you: for the seal of mine apostleship are ye in the Lord [1 Cor. 9:2].

"If I be not an apostle unto others"—but he was an apostle to others. The "if" is the *if* of condition.

"Yet doubtless I am to you: for the seal of mine apostleship are ye in the Lord."

As far as the Corinthian church was concerned, he didn't have to defend his apostleship. It was evident to the Christians there that he was an apostle.

Mine answer to them that do examine me is this,

Have we not power to eat and to drink? [1 Cor. 9:3-4].

The word for "answer" in the Greek really means *defense*. It is as if Paul were in court and were being charged concerning his apostleship. He is giving his defense to those who examine him. What is his defense?

"Have we not power to eat and to drink?" As an apostle of the Lord Jesus Christ, Paul had a right to eat and to drink. As an apostle he had that liberty. However, that liberty is curbed and curtailed by others. He had made the bold declaration. "Wherefore, if meat make my brother to offend, I will eat no flesh while the world standeth, lest I make my brother to offend" (1 Cor. 8:13). He had the right to eat meat, but he was not going to eat meat. Now that is an exercise of free will, isn't it? It is free will to be able to do something and then choose not to do it. In a sense, that is a higher liberty, perhaps the highest liberty that there is. If you cannot do something, you do not do it; there is no exercise of free will in that. But if you are able to do something and then choose not to do it, that is a revelation of your free will.

Have we not power to lead about a sister, a wife, as well as other apostles, and as the brethren of the Lord, and Cephas? [1 Cor. 9:5].

Evidently "the brethren of the Lord" refers to the half brothers of Jesus, James and Jude, who were apparently married. And Peter was married. They took their wives with them when they went out on their missionary journeys. Paul says that he has the same freedom, but he chose not to have a wife because he felt his ministry would be curtailed and hindered.

Today in Bible conference work if you take your wife, they wonder whether you can't go anywhere without her. If you don't take your wife, they wonder what is wrong. A preacher is in a bad way. When my daughter was growing up, my wife stayed at home to take care of her, and I would go alone to the Bible conferences. I would be quizzed by some of the curious saints, and I would have to go into detail to explain why Mrs. McGee wasn't with me. Now my daughter is grown and married, so my wife goes everywhere with me. Every now and then one of the saints asks, "Does your wife go with you *all* the time?" as if to say, "Can't you ever get away from her?" In the ministry you will be questioned regardless of what you do.

Paul faced this same sort of thing. Paul says that he has the right to take a wife with him—he has that liberty—but he has made his decision to remain single. After all, he was a pioneer missionary, and his was a very rugged life.

> **Or I only and Barnabas, have not we power to forbear working? [1 Cor. 9:6].**

He is saying that he and Barnabas could stay home if they wished. In other words, "We don't have to go as missionaries—our salvation wouldn't be affected if we stayed home."

Now he is going to get around to this matter of paying the preacher.

> **Who goeth a warfare any time at his own charges? who planteth a vineyard, and eateth not of the fruit thereof? or who feedeth a flock, and eateth not of the milk of the flock?**
>
> **Say I these things as a man? or saith not the law the same also?**
>
> **For it is written in the law of Moses, Thou shalt not muzzle the mouth of the ox that treadeth out the corn. Doth God take care for oxen? [1 Cor. 9:7–9].**

In those days an ox was used to tread out the corn. They hitched the ox to a horizontal wheel, and he walked around in a circle over the grain. This separated the grain from the chaff. Then the chaff was pitched up into the air so the wind would blow it away, and the good grain would fall down onto the threshing floor. God said they were not to muzzle the ox that was treading out the grain. Why? He was working and was to be permitted to eat the grain as he worked. That was the way God took care of the ox—He made that a law. The application is that the preacher is not to be muzzled. He is to be fed for his work.

I heard a story about a preacher in Kentucky who drove a very fine, beautiful horse, but the preacher himself was a very skinny fellow. One day one of his church officers asked him the question (which had been a matter of discussion), "How is it, preacher, that your horse is so fine looking and you are such a skinny fellow?" The preacher answered, "I will tell you. I feed my horse, and you are the ones who feed me."

God says not to muzzle the ox that is working for you, and Paul applies that principle to pastors and teachers. God not only cares for oxen, He cares for preachers. Paul is saying that he, as an apostle who has fed others, has a right to be fed.

> Or saith he it altogether for our sakes? For our sakes, no doubt, this is written: that he that ploweth should plow in hope; and that he that thresheth in hope should be partaker of his hope.

> If we have sown unto you spiritual things, is it a great thing if we shall reap your carnal things? [1 Cor. 9:10–11].

Paul mentions this again in the Epistle to the Galatians. If folk have given you spiritual blessings, spiritual riches, then you should share your carnal blessings with them. I heard Torrey Johnson down in Bibletown in Florida say several times—and I think it is a good principle—that you ought to support the place where you get your blessing. Suppose you go down to eat at a certain restaurant. You don't walk down the street and around the corner into another restaurant to pay your bill; you pay the restaurant that fed you. Yet many people do that sort of thing with their spiritual food. They get their spiritual blessings in one place, and they give their offerings in another place.

> If others be partakers of this power over you, are not we rather? Nevertheless we have not used this power; but suffer all things, lest we should hinder the gospel of Christ [1 Cor. 9:12].

Paul has a right to be supported for his work. Yet, he doesn't want to do anything that would hinder the gospel of Christ. Therefore he doesn't receive any remuneration; he supports himself by plying his trade, which is tentmaking.

In our day there are many religious rackets. To say there are not is to be as blind as a bat. Unfortunately, there are men who make merchandise of the gospel of Christ—there is no doubt about it. However, it is God's method that those who have a spiritual ministry are to be supported by those who benefit.

> **Do ye not know that they which minister about holy things live of the things of the temple? and they which wait at the altar are partakers with the altar? [1 Cor. 9:13].**

That is God's method.

> **Even so hath the Lord ordained that they which preach the gospel should live of the gospel [1 Cor. 9:14].**

It is not wrong for the minister who has been a blessing to his people to be supported by the people. I have discovered that, when people receive a blessing, for the most part they will support the place where they get their blessing.

> **But I have used none of these things: neither have I written these things, that it should be so done unto me: for it were better for me to die, than that any man should make my glorying void [1 Cor. 9:15].**

You see, Paul did not take a salary. He was able to say that the church in Corinth was not supporting him; he didn't receive anything from them. Paul supported himself by tentmaking.

> **For though I preach the gospel, I have nothing to glory of: for necessity is laid upon me; yea, woe is unto me, if I preach not the gospel! [1 Cor. 9:16].**

I understand Paul's feeling. To be frank with you, necessity is laid on me also. I dare not stop giving out the Word of God. Of course, I would not lose my salvation if I stopped, but I continue because I feel an inner compulsion, and also I love to teach and preach the gospel.

> For if I do this thing willingly, I have a reward: but if
> against my will, a dispensation of the gospel is commit-
> ted unto me.

> What is my reward then? Verily that, when I preach the
> gospel, I may make the gospel of Christ without charge,
> that I abuse not my power in the gospel [1 Cor. 9:17–18].

Paul did not preach the gospel for an ulterior motive and neither do I.
Yet God has promised a reward. I know we will not be disappointed.

> For though I be free from all men, yet have I made my-
> self servant unto all, that I might gain the more [1 Cor.
> 9:19].

He had the freedom to make himself a servant!
Now he gives this very familiar testimony of his own ministry.

> And unto the Jews I became as a Jew, that I might gain
> the Jews; to them that are under the law, as under the
> law, that I might gain them that are under the law;

> To them that are without law, as without law, (being not
> without law to God, but under the law to Christ,) that I
> might gain them that are without law.

> To the weak became I as weak, that I might gain the
> weak: I am made all things to all men, that I might by
> all means save some.

> And this I do for the gospel's sake, that I might be par-
> taker thereof with you [1 Cor. 9:20–23].

Paul says, "I'm doing all of this because I am out on the racetrack. I am
like an athlete out there running." Running for what? A prize.

> Know ye not that they which run in a race run all, but
> one receiveth the prize? So run, that ye may obtain
> [1 Cor. 9:24].

In an athletic event, only one can come in first. But in the spiritual race all of us can win the prize if we are getting out the Word of God.

And every man that striveth for the mastery is temperate in all things. Now they do it to obtain a corruptible crown; but we an incorruptible [1 Cor. 9:25].

The awards that God gives won't swell your bank account down here and remain here when you leave; they will be for your eternal enrichment.

I therefore so run, not as uncertainly: so fight I, not as one that beateth the air [1 Cor. 9:26].

Paul says that he is not just shadowboxing. He is not just playing at this thing. He is not playing church. This is real.

But I keep under my body, and bring it into subjection: lest that by any means, when I have preached to others, I myself should be a castaway [1 Cor. 9:27].

The translation "castaway" is unfortunate. Thr Greek word is *adokimos*, which means "not approved." Paul is thinking of the judgment seat of Christ where the rewards are given. In his Second Epistle to the Corinthians he will talk about the fact that we shall all appear before the judgment seat of Christ where awards are given. Paul says that he is out on that racetrack trying to run so that he will get a reward. That is the reason he preaches the gospel as he does. Paul has liberty. This is the choice that he has made.

I think every Christian ought to work for a reward. We do not work for salvation; that is a gift given by the grace of God. My friend, if you are going to get a reward, you will have to work for it. If you are going to get a reward, then you had better get out on the racetrack and start moving.

CHAPTER 10

THEME: Liberty is not license

W e are still in the section concerning Christian liberty, which extends through this chapter and into the first verse of chapter 11. We are going to see another area of liberty illustrated through the nation Israel.

> **Moreover, brethren, I would not that ye should be ignorant, how that all our fathers were under the cloud, and all passed through the sea [1 Cor. 10:1].**

"Moreover, brethren" ties into the last verse of chapter 9. Paul had just been saying that he did not want to be disapproved at the judgment seat of Christ, but he wanted to receive a reward.

"I would not that ye should be ignorant." When Paul writes that, you can be sure that the brethren were ignorant or unaware of something he is going to explain to them.

The church in Corinth was a mixed church; that is, it was made up of both Jews and Gentiles. Today a Jewish Christian is somewhat unusual, but in that day a Gentile Christian was more unusual since the first Christians were Jews.

When Paul says, "All our fathers," he is speaking to the Jewish part of the congregation. They, along with Paul, were Israelites and shared the same history.

"Our fathers were under the cloud, and all passed through the sea" refers, of course, to the time when the people of Israel were escaping from Egyptian bondage and crossed the Red Sea.

> **And were all baptized unto Moses in the cloud and in the sea;**
>
> **And did all eat the same spiritual meat;**

And did all drink the same spiritual drink: for they drank of that spiritual Rock that followed them: and that Rock was Christ.

But with many of them God was not well pleased: for they were overthrown in the wilderness [1 Cor. 10:2–5].

"Many of them" is in the Greek "*most* of them."

This shows how far a person can go and still not be a believer. It reveals the wonderful liberty the Israelites had when they crossed the Red Sea. The Mosaic Law had not been given at that time; so they were not under law. They had great liberty, but they abused that liberty. Privilege is no insurance against ultimate failure. Many a rich man's son has had to learn that. It has also been learned by many men who had certain privileges granted them in the political realm or in the business world or in the social world.

They "were under the cloud"—that is, they had guidance. They all passed safely through the sea.

They "were all baptized unto Moses." Here we come again to that word *baptized*. *Baptized* can mean many things. I have a classical Greek lexicon which gives twenty meanings for the Greek word *baptizō*. Our translators never did translate the word; they merely transliterated it. They simply took the word out of the Greek and gave it an English spelling. Therefore, to try to say exactly what the writer had in mind is difficult because the translators did not attempt to do that. They just spelled the word out. A great many folk have dogmatically narrowed down the word to one meaning.

Now *baptizō* means to "identify." In fact, water baptism has that meaning, as it speaks of our identification with Christ. We are buried with Him by baptism—by the baptism of the Holy Spirit—that is what the baptism of the Holy Spirit is. He identifies us with the body of Christ—He puts us into the body as a member. "For by one Spirit are we all baptized into one body" (1 Cor. 12:13). Paul will deal with this in chapter 12.

But here we have the statement that they were "baptized unto Moses." How were they baptized unto Moses? Don't try to tell me that Moses had a baptismal service at the Red Sea and baptized them because, actually, they did not get wet at all! The record in Exodus tells us that they went through the sea on dry ground. When God dried up the Red Sea for them, He dried it up—they didn't get wet at all. They went over on dry land. The folk who really got wet were the Egyptians. They were soaked through and through. So obviously when it says they were baptized unto Moses, he is not talking about water. Neither is it the baptism of the Holy Spirit because it says they were baptized unto *Moses*. Well, it simply means that they were *identified* with Moses. Hebrews 11:29 says, "By faith they passed through the Red sea as by dry land: which the Egyptians assaying to do were drowned." The children of Israel were identified with Moses. By faith they passed through the Red Sea. Whose faith was it? It wasn't their faith. They had none. Read the story in Exodus—they wanted to go back to Egypt, and they were blaming Moses for bringing them out into that awful wilderness. It was *Moses* who had the faith. It was *Moses* who went down to the water and smote the Red Sea as God had commanded. It was *Moses* who led them across on dry ground. When they got to the other side, they sang the song of Moses (see Exod. 15). What a song it was! The people of Israel were identified with Moses.

All of this is a picture of our salvation. Christ went through the waters of death. And we are brought through by His death, identified with Him, and now identified with a living Savior, baptized into Christ. That is the way baptism saves us. When we trust Christ, the baptism of the Holy Spirit puts us in Christ.

Water baptism illustrates this and is very important, but it is merely ritual baptism. *Real* baptism is the work of the Holy Spirit.

Now the people of Israel were baptized unto Moses, and they were able to cross the Red Sea. "And did all eat the same spiritual meat"—the manna. "And did all drink the same spiritual drink: for they drank of that spiritual Rock that followed them: and that Rock was Christ"—that is, it sets forth Christ.

"But with most of them God was not well pleased: for they were overthrown in the wilderness."

Why was all of this recorded for us? Paul tells us the reason:

Now these things were our examples, to the intent we

should not lust after evil things, as they also lusted [1 Cor. 10:6].

The first five verses give us the illustration of the liberty that these people enjoyed as a nation. Now in this very searching section we learn that these people abused their liberty. He makes an application of that for us. It happened to them for examples unto us. This was written for you and for me, and so we ought to pay close attention to it. The Israelites had this wonderful liberty, and what did they do with it?

It says that they lusted after evil things. What were those things? Well, we can turn back and see: "And the mixed multitude that was among them fell a-lusting: and the children of Israel also wept again, and said, Who shall give us flesh to eat? We remember the fish, which we did eat in Egypt freely; the cucumbers, and the melons, and the leeks, and the onions, and the garlick: But now our soul is dried away: there is nothing at all, beside this manna, before our eyes" (Num. 11:4–6). They lusted, we are told, after *evil* things. What was wrong with leeks, onions, and garlic? Well, if they ate those things, they wouldn't be very desirable companions, but the point is that they lusted for that which was outside the will of God for them. This was the beginning of their defection.

Have you noticed how many times it is desire that leads to sin? It started back in the Garden of Eden. "And when the woman saw that the tree was good for food, and that it was pleasant to the eyes, and a tree to be desired to make one wise, she took of the fruit thereof, and did eat, and gave also unto her husband with her, and he did eat" (Gen. 3:6). It was the desire for something outside the will of God. What is desire, after all? Psychologists talk about inhibitions and prohibitions, and they speak of desire as the supreme thing in life. What is desire? In these instances it was to want that which was outside the will of God. It wasn't God's will for them to have those things at that particular time.

Neither be ye idolaters, as were some of them; as it is written, The people sat down to eat and drink, and rose up to play [1 Cor. 10:7].

An idol is anything in your life that you put in the place of God.

> **Neither let us commit fornication, as some of them committed, and fell in one day three and twenty thousand.**
>
> **Neither let us tempt Christ, as some of them also tempted, and were destroyed of serpents.**
>
> **Neither murmur ye, as some of them also murmured, and were destroyed of the destroyer [1 Cor. 10:8–10].**

Paul lists some of the sins of the people. These people had continually murmured and complained against God. This is an illustration of those who want those things that are outside the will of God. God always has something good for His people. That was true then, and it is still true now. But they constantly wanted something that was beyond God's will for them.

> **Now all these things happened unto them for ensamples: and they are written for our admonition, upon whom the ends of the world are come [1 Cor. 10:11].**

We are to learn a lesson from all this. We do have Christian liberty, but our desires are to be according to the will of God. That is so important for us to see.

> **Wherefore let him that thinketh he standeth take heed lest he fall [1 Cor. 10:12].**

It makes no difference who you are, you could fall today. It would be very easy for any one of us to blunder and stumble and fall. One can be a mature Christian, a real saint, and still fall. Therefore, you and I need to be very careful that we stay in the realm of the will of God where we are not quenching the Spirit of God in our lives.

> **There hath no temptation taken you but such as is common to man: but God is faithful, who will not suffer you**

to be tempted above that ye are able; but will with the temptation also make a way to escape, that ye may be able to bear it [1 Cor. 10:13].

A great many people feel that nobody has ever been tempted as they are tempted. My friend, no matter what temptation you experience, there have been others who have had the same kind of temptation. The encouraging thing is that God will make a way of escape for you. God is faithful; He will not let you be tempted beyond what you can endure.

Dr. Hutton used to say it like this: "God always makes a way of escape and sometimes the way of escape is the king's highway and a good pair of heels." In other words, let the Devil see your heels—run as hard as you can to get away from the temptation. One of the reasons we yield to temptation is that we are like the little boy in the pantry. His mother heard a noise because he had taken down the cookie jar. She said, "Willie, where are you?" He answered that he was in the pantry. "What are you doing there?" He said, "I'm fighting temptation." My friend, that is not the place to fight temptation! That is the place to start running.

Wherefore, my dearly beloved, flee from idolatry.

I speak as to wise men; judge ye what I say [1 Cor. 10:14–15].

Idolatry was a temptation in Corinth. Idolatry may not be a temptation to you, but the Bible tells us that covetousness is idolatry. There is a lot of that around today.

Paul is going on to teach that fellowship at the Lord's Table requires separation.

The cup of blessing which we bless, is it not the communion of the blood of Christ? The bread which we break, is it not the communion of the body of Christ?

For we being many are one bread, and one body: for we are all partakers of that one bread.

> Behold Israel after the flesh: are not they which eat of the sacrifices partakers of the altar?
>
> What say I then? that the idol is any thing, or that which is offered in sacrifice to idols is any thing? [1 Cor. 10:16–19].

Paul's argument here is quite logical. He says that an idol is nothing. So if you offer meat to an idol, it is nothing—the meat is not affected at all.

> But I say, that the things which the Gentiles sacrifice, they sacrifice to devils, and not to God: and I would not that ye should have fellowship with devils [1 Cor. 10:20].

Paul is still talking about Christian liberty. Although the idol is nothing, behind the idol is demonism—Paul recognizes this.

> Ye cannot drink the cup of the Lord, and the cup of devils: ye cannot be partakers of the Lord's table, and of the table of devils [1 Cor. 10:21].

That is, for some people to eat meat which had been sacrificed to idols *would* be idolatry. A believer would have to examine his heart very carefully.

> Do we provoke the Lord to jealousy? are we stronger than he? [1 Cor. 10:22].

Paul now comes back to what he said at the very beginning of this section on Christian liberty.

> All things are lawful for me, but all things are not expedient: all things are lawful for me, but all things edify not [1 Cor. 10:23].

Paul says that he has the freedom to do these questionable things, things on which the Bible is silent as to their being right or wrong. For example, I think Paul would say, "If I felt that I should go to the games, I would go." I think Paul must have attended the great Olympic events which took place in his day because many of his illustrations are taken from athletic events that were carried on in the great Colosseum and stadiums of that day. Paul says all such things are lawful for him, but all things are not expedient because of the fact that the thing he could do might hurt a weak believer. He says, "All things are lawful for me, but all things edify not." That is, they don't "build me up in the faith."

A young preacher once asked me, "Do you think a preacher ought to go to ball games?" He knew I didn't go. I said this to him, "Although I always enjoyed participating in all athletic events, I've never been much of a spectator at any of them. I don't have much interest in watching somebody else play football or baseball, especially when they are being paid for it. I always played for fun and enjoyed it. However, when I was in school, I read a very helpful book which pointed out that a preacher should confine his life to that which he can use in his ministry—what he sees, where he goes, what he experiences—because his total life is his ministry. Everything should be grist for his mill. In other words, a minister should take into the pulpit his entire life (he is not to have a hidden part) and be able to use all of it." So I said to him regarding baseball, "If you can use the baseball game—and you can—there would be nothing wrong in your going. You could draw many good illustrations from a baseball game. However, it might not be expedient for you to go because it might have a bad influence on someone else."

So Paul lays down this guideline:

Let no man seek his own, but every man another's wealth [1 Cor. 10:24].

The Christian has a tremendous liberty in Christ. However, we are to seek the welfare of the other man. So a Christian's life should not be primarily directed and dictated by liberty. Liberty is limited by love.

A Christian is not pinned down by legality; he is not circumscribed by strict rules. He is limited by love. He should be concerned about his influence and effect on others. That is the thought which Paul has here.

> **Whatsoever is sold in the shambles, that eat, asking no question for conscience sake:**
>
> **For the earth is the Lord's, and the fulness thereof [1 Cor. 10:25–26].**

The Christian can enjoy all the things of God's creation—the beauties of it and the produce of it. The Lord has provided it.

Now Paul is going to give a very practical suggestion. He says that when you go out to eat, don't say to your host, "This is a very lovely steak that you have here today. Where did you get it? My butcher doesn't have meat like this to sell to the public." Then your friend may tell you that he went to the temple to buy the meat. The best thing to do is not to ask where the meat came from.

Now Paul gives a very practical illustration:

> **If any of them that believe not bid you to a feast, and ye be disposed to go; whatsoever is set before you, eat, asking no question for conscience sake [1 Cor. 10:27].**

If you are invited to the home of an unbeliever, go and eat whatever is put before you. Don't ask any questions.

> **But if any man say unto you, This is offered in sacrifice unto idols, eat not for his sake that shewed it, and for conscience sake: for the earth is the Lord's, and the fulness thereof [1 Cor. 10:28].**

Now there is another principle involved, and this is an entirely new matter. Paul has advised to eat everything and ask no questions. But suppose there is someone else at the table who sees you eat the meat and says, "This meat has been offered to idols." In that case you should not eat the meat—not because eating it is wrong, but because it is obvious it may harm the person who pointed it out to you. It is not because of your conscience but because of *his* conscience that you should not eat the meat. There is no rule that you should not eat the meat. But out of your love, out of your desire to help that brother whose conscience is bothered, you should not eat the meat. That is the whole point.

Let me illustrate this. Down in Georgia they have a berry that is called a scuppernong. It is similar to a grape, but it grows singly on a vine. They make wine out of it. A friend of mine told me that he went to preach in a certain church and was invited out to dinner by one of the church officers. He was handed a glass of scuppernong. He didn't know what it was, but he tasted of it. He realized that it had an alcoholic content—he is not a super pious individual, but he put the glass down. His host said to him, "What's the matter? Don't you like it?" He said, "I think it is delicious, but I noticed that it is wine, and I feel that I as a Christian should not drink it." Well, that created a tense moment, but he got his point across. I feel that he did the right thing.

The question would arise: did that minister have as much right to drink it as the elder did? He did—there's no question about that. But he also had a testimony, which is the reason he did not drink it. So many Christians are harsh in their dealing with others because their motive is legality—"I don't do this, and you shouldn't do it." However, if their motive were love, the approach would be altogether different. Love for the other believer should be the motive in the Christian's conduct.

> **Conscience, I say, not thine own, but of the other: for why is my liberty judged of another man's conscience? [1 Cor. 10:29].**

Why should I be restricted by some of these weak brethren?

> **For if I by grace be a partaker, why am I evil spoken of for that for which I give thanks? [1 Cor. 10:30].**

Paul asks, "Isn't it unfair to judge me because of another man's conscience?" He answers by stating a great principle:

Whether therefore ye eat, or drink, or whatsoever ye do, do all to the glory of God [1 Cor. 10:31].

Paul has stated certain great principles that relate to Christian liberty. One of those principles is: "All things are lawful for me, but all things are not expedient." Also, "all things are lawful for me, but all things edify not." Now here is another one: "Whether therefore ye eat, or drink, and whatsoever ye do, do all to the glory of God." This is the test every believer should apply to his life. Not "should I do this, or should I do that," but "can I do it for the glory of God?" Unfortunately, there are Christians who don't even go to church for the glory of God. They go for some other reason—maybe to criticize or to gossip. With a motive like that it is better to stay at home. Whatever a believer does should be done for the glory of God. That is very important.

Give none offence, neither to the Jews, nor to the Gentiles, nor to the church of God [1 Cor. 10:32].

Here Paul divides the whole world into three groups: Jews, Gentiles, and church of God. Some of these folk have differing beliefs. An example would be the Jewish abhorrence of pork. It would certainly give offense to invite a Jewish friend for dinner and serve him ham. A believer should love other people enough so that his actions will not offend them. There are a lot of Gentiles who have peculiar notions too. It would be impossible to please all of them, but we should try not to offend those with whom we have contact. Neither should we offend those who are of the church of God. Some young people who were rebelling against "the establishment" came to me and said they had attended a certain church and were rebuked because of the way they dressed. They asked me if I thought the members of that church were all wrong. I told them I thought that both groups were wrong. Neither acted in love. The members of the church were wrong in criticizing them before others. On the other hand, these young folk knew their clothes and hair would be an offense to the members of the church. So none of them showed love toward the other. We are told that we are not to offend either the Jews, the Gentiles, or the church of God. This includes the entire human family. These are the three divisions of the human family today, but one of these days the church of God is going to leave this earth. Then there will be only the Jews and Gentiles in the world, and God has a tremendous program which will take place at that time.

Even as I please all men in all things, not seeking mine own profit, but the profit of many, that they may be saved [1 Cor. 10:33].

Now primarily what we do we are to do for the glory of God—"Whether therefore ye eat, or drink, or whatsoever ye do, do all to the glory of God." A Christian woman can wash dishes and sweep the floor to the glory of God. A Christian man can mow the lawn and dig a ditch for the glory of God. Regardless of what you are doing, if you cannot do it for the glory of God, you should not be doing it. As we live like this we are a testimony to the world—that those who are lost might be saved.

Friend, it is more important for us to make tracks in the world than to give out tracts. A zealous man in Memphis, Tennessee, was handing out tracts to everyone. He handed a tract to a man, but he would not accept it. He asked, "What is that?" "A tract," was the answer. "I can't read," said the man, "but I'll tell you what I'll do, I'll just watch your tracks." That is much more impressive. People read our tracks in life better than they read tracts that we hand out. It is a good thing to give out tracts, but along with them we must also make the right kind of tracks.

Now the first verse of chapter 11 belongs in this division:

Be ye followers of me, even as I also am of Christ [1 Cor. 11:1].

This is something that very few of us can say. Well, I shouldn't include you, but it is something that I dare not say. I want you to be a follower of Christ and a follower of Paul—but don't follow me in everything. What a tremendous testimony Paul gives in that statement!

CHAPTER 11

We have concluded the section concerning Christian liberty, which extended from chapter 8 to the first verse of this chapter. Now Paul is dealing with other matters about which the Corinthian church had written him.

Someone is probably saying, "Do you mean to say that God is giving instructions regarding trivialities like a woman's dress? Certainly God cannot be concerned with what a woman wears or whether a man gets a hair cut!" Well, the Bible makes it clear that God is interested in what we are wearing and how we fix our hair. God says, "But the very hairs of your head are all numbered" (Matt. 10:30). This idea that only your hairdresser knows is not true; God knows, my friend. He has a great deal to say about these and related subjects. The most intimate details of our lives are under His inspection. There is probably no single item that takes up more space in newspapers, magazines, radio time, and television time than what men and women wear. The Word of God has some things to say about that, too.

WOMEN'S DRESS

Now I praise you, brethren, that ye remember me in all things, and keep the ordinances, as I delivered them to you [1 Cor. 11:2].

Up to this point he had said, "I praise you not," but here Paul has an item of praise for them. He praises them because they have remembered him in prayer and in their giving, and they were practicing the ordinances he had taught them.

But I would have you know, that the head of every man is Christ; and the head of the woman is the man; and the head of Christ is God [1 Cor. 11:3].

I realize full well that there are people today who like to emphasize the middle statement: "the head of the woman is the man." But, my friend, when you put all these statements together, you don't come up with a lopsided viewpoint. Paul is putting down another great principle here: This is authority for the sake of order, to eliminate confusion.

This principle is important in the church as well as the home. Several years ago a pastor was having trouble in his church, and I asked him what the problem was. He said it was that he had too many chiefs and not enough Indians—everyone wanted to be a leader. Today we find churches which have courses in leadership training. I'd like to know where you find that in the Bible. There are organizations which exist solely for the purpose of training young people to be public speakers. Paul says we are to "study to be quiet" (1 Thess. 4:11). I wish we could put the emphasis where the Bible puts it. We don't need all this leadership training. We need folk who will act and live like Christians. That is the important thing.

The important word here is *head*. "The head of every man is Christ; and the head of the woman is the man; and the head of Christ is God." The head is that portion of the body that gives the direction.

This verse does not say that the head of every *Christian* man is Christ. The word *man* is generic—it is a general item. It says the head of *every* man is Christ. It is the normal and correct order for Christ to be the head of every man. Until a man is mastered by Christ, he is not a normal man. Some men are mastered by drink; some are mastered by passion; most are mastered by the flesh. Every man should be mastered by *Christ*. Augustine said, "The heart of man is restless until it finds its rest in thee" (*Confessions*, Bk. 1, sec. 1). The heart of man is restless until he makes Christ the head. Men who have accomplished great things for God have done this. I think of Martin Luther and Wilberforce and Augustine who were profligate until they were mastered by Christ. I hear it said of a man today, "He is a Christian man." Is he mastered by Christ? That is the important thing, and that is what Paul is saying.

"The head of the woman is man"—there is no article in the Greek, it is not *the* man. Notice it is not *every* woman; it is not an absolute. It refers to marriage where the woman is to respond to the man. It is normal for the woman to be subject to the man in marriage. If a woman cannot look up to a man and respect him, she ought not to follow him and surely ought not to marry him. But a real woman responds with every fiber of her being to the man she loves. He, in turn, must be the man who is willing to *die* for her—"Husbands, love your wives, even as Christ also loved the church, and gave himself for it" (Eph. 5:25).

Dr. G. Campbell Morgan told about a friend of his and his wife's who was a very brilliant woman. She had a strong personality, was an outstanding person, and was not married. He asked her one day the pointed question, "Why have you never married?" Her answer was, "I have never found a man who could master me." So she never married. May I say that until a woman finds that man, she would make a mistake to get married. If she marries a Mr. Milquetoast, she will be in trouble from that day on.

"The head of Christ is God." There is a great mystery here. Jesus said, "I and my Father are one" (John 10:30), but He also said, ". . . for my Father is greater than I" (John 14:28). In the work of redemption, He voluntarily took a lower place and was made lower than the angels. He walked a lowly path down here. We are admonished, "Let this mind be in you, which was also in Christ Jesus: Who, being in the form of God, thought it not robbery to be equal with God: But made himself of no reputation, and took upon him the form of a servant, and was made in the likeness of men" (Phil. 2:5–7).

Now Paul is going to apply this principle of headship to the situation in Corinth. An unveiled woman in Corinth was a prostitute. The situation in your church or in your community may be different than it was in Corinth, but there is a principle here and it still applies today.

Every man praying or prophesying, having his head covered, dishonoureth his head [1 Cor. 11:4].

The rabbis of that day taught that a man was to cover his head. Paul says that they actually misinterpreted Moses and the reason for the veil. "And not as Moses, which put a veil over his face, that the children of Israel could not stedfastly look to the end of that which is abolished" (2 Cor. 3:13). This refers to an experience Moses had when he came down from the mount where he had communed with God. When he first came down, the skin of his face shone, but after awhile that glory began to disappear. Therefore, he covered his face so they wouldn't discover the glory was disappearing (see Exod. 34:33–35).

Paul is saying to the men that they ought *not* to cover their heads. A man created in the image of God, who is in Christ by redemption, is to have his head uncovered as a symbol of dignity and of liberty. He is not to be covered when he prays or when he prophesies. When he is praying, he is speaking for man to God, making intercession. When he is prophesying, he is speaking for God to man. Whenever he is standing in these two sacred, holy positions, he is to have his head uncovered.

> **But every woman that prayeth or prophesieth with her head uncovered dishonoureth her head: for that is even all one as if she were shaven [1 Cor. 11:5].**

They had a woman's liberation movement going in Corinth centuries ago, and it was going in the wrong direction. Paul says that the man should have his head uncovered but that the woman should have her head covered.

I want you to note that it says "every woman that prayeth or prophesieth," which means that a woman can pray in public and it means she can speak in public. Folk who maintain that the Bible says a woman cannot do these things are entirely wrong. The woman has the right to do these things if God has given her that gift. Some women have the gift.

I know several women today who are outstanding Bible teachers. They can out-teach any man. One preacher told me this very candidly, "My wife is a much better Bible teacher than I am." An officer of the church said they would much rather hear her speak than hear him speak. She had the gift of teaching.

> **For if the woman be not covered, let her also be shorn: but if it be a shame for a woman to be shorn or shaven, let her be covered [1 Cor. 11:6].**

This had a peculiar and particular application to Corinth. The unveiled woman in Corinth was a prostitute. Many of them had their heads shaved. The vestal virgins in the temple of Aphrodite who were really prostitutes had their heads shaved. The women who had their heads uncovered were the prostitutes. Apparently some of the women in the church at Corinth were saying, "All things are lawful for me, therefore, I won't cover my head." Paul says this should not be done because the veil is a mark of subjection, not to man, but to God. Now this had a local application; it was given to the women in Corinth. Does it apply to our day and society? Well, I have heard that a new hat is a morale builder for women. A wife said to her husband, "Every time I get down in the dumps, I go and buy a new hat." His response was, "I have been wondering where you got those hats!" Seriously, regulations for a woman's dress are in regard to her ministry. If she is to lead, she ought to have her head covered. Other passages will give us more information about this. "I will therefore that men pray every where, lifting up holy hands, without wrath and doubting. In like manner also, that women adorn themselves in modest apparel, with shamefacedness and sobriety; not with broided hair, or gold, or pearls, or costly array; But (which becometh women professing godliness) with good works" (1 Tim. 2:8–10). This states that if the woman is to lift up holy hands in the service in leading, she is not to adorn herself to draw attention to herself. Very candidly, it means that the woman is not to use sex appeal in the service of God. That is exactly what it means, my friend. She is not to use sex appeal at all—it will not win her husband to Christ either.

The Bible has more to say on this subject. "Likewise, ye wives, be in subjection to your own husbands; that, if any obey not the word, they also may without the word be won by the conversation of the wives. . . . Whose adorning let it not be that outward adorning of plaiting the hair, and of wearing of gold, or of putting on of apparel; But let it be the hidden man of the heart, in that which is not corruptible, even the ornament of a meek and quiet spirit, which is in the sight of God of great price" (1 Pet. 3:1, 3–4). God is saying that a wife cannot win her husband to Christ by sex appeal. This does not mean that she is not to be appealing to her husband, but it does mean that a woman never wins her husband to Christ by sex appeal. There are women in the Bible who had sex appeal: Jezebel, Esther, Salome. Then there are some who stand out in Scripture as being wonderful, marvelous, godly women whom God used: Sarah, Deborah, Hannah, Abigail, and Mary the mother of Jesus. Then there is also something said to the husbands. "Likewise, ye husbands, dwell with them according to knowledge, giving honour unto the wife, as unto the weaker vessel, and as being heirs together of the grace of life; that your prayers be not hindered" (1 Pet. 3:7). Many a family today have their prayers hindered because the husband and wife are not getting along as they should.

Now Paul goes back to the principle he laid down for men in verse 4.

> **For a man indeed ought not to cover his head, forasmuch as he is the image and glory of God: but the woman is the glory of the man.**

> **For the man is not of the women; but the woman of the man.**

> **Neither was the man created for the woman; but the woman for the man [1 Cor. 11:7-9].**

The woman's place is to be a helpmeet to the man. She is to be the other part of him. No man is complete without a woman except where God has given special grace to a man for a special work. Listen to the next verse.

> **For this cause ought the woman to have power on her head because of the angels [1 Cor. 11:10].**

Now here is a reference to angels that I don't understand. I am of the opinion that we are being observed by God's created intelligences. We are on a stage in this little world, and all God's created intelligences are watching us. They are finding out about the love of God because they know we are not worthy of the love of God. They probably think

God would have done well to have gotten rid of us because we are rebellious creatures in His universe. But He didn't! He loves us! That display of His love is in His grace to save us. The angels probably marvel at His grace and patience with little man.

Nevertheless neither is the man without the woman, neither the woman without the man, in the Lord [1 Cor. 11:11].

The power of the woman is to hold her man because she is a woman. The man holds his woman because he is a man. This is the marriage relationship as God ordained it. When that relationship doesn't exist, then God's ideal is lost.

For as the woman is of the man, even so is the man also by the woman; but all things of God [1 Cor. 11:12].

They are inseparable. Man is not a sphere but a hemisphere; woman is not a sphere but a hemisphere. It is nonsense for either men or women to talk about liberation. The man needs the woman, and the woman needs the man. This is true liberty in the glorious relationship of marriage.

Judge in yourselves: is it comely that a woman pray unto God uncovered? [1 Cor. 11:13].

A woman ought not to call attention to herself when she is speaking for the Lord or teaching a Bible class or praying. There should be no sex appeal. Also, she needs to remember that her sex appeal is a tremendous thing which has the power to either lift a man up or drag him down.

Doth not even nature itself teach you, that, if a man have long hair, it is a shame unto him? [1 Cor. 11:14].

As I write this, long hair is a fad among men. Men who let their hair grow so long that you can hardly recognize them seem to me to be expressing a lack of purpose in life. I wonder if it is a movement toward the animal world. Notice that Paul asks, "Doth not even nature itself teach you, that, if a man have long hair, it is a shame unto him?" We have an example of this in the Old Testament. The Nazarite vow was an act of consecrating oneself to God. It was symbolized by long, uncut hair. This meant that a Nazarite was willing to bear shame for God's name. Even at that time men's long hair was considered shameful.

But if a woman have long hair, it is a glory to her: for her hair is given her for a covering [1 Cor. 11:15].

Now it is true that today we have liberty in Christ. The length of the hair is really not so much the issue as the motive behind it. Many men wear long hair as a sign of rebellion, and many women cut their hair as a sign of rebellion. Our moral values get turned upside down, and there is a danger of being an extremist in either direction.

Extremism leads to strange behavior like the lady who went to the psychiatrist because her family had urged her to go. The psychiatrist asked her, "What really seems to be your trouble?" She said, "They think it is strange that I like pancakes." He answered, "There is nothing wrong in liking pancakes. I like pancakes myself." So she said, "You do? Well, come over sometime; I have trunks filled with them!" You see, my friend, you can be an extremist in that which is a normal thing.

Now Paul says that it is not really the haircut or the style of the dress that is of utmost importance.

But if any man seem to be contentious, we have no such custom, neither the churches of God [1 Cor. 11:16].

Paul concludes by saying that the church ought not to make rules in connection with the matter of women's dress or men's hair. The really important issue is the inner man. It is the old nature which needs a haircut and the robe of righteousness. My friend, if we are clothed with the robe of Christ's righteousness and if our old nature is under the control of the Holy Spirit, that will take care of the outer man. The haircut and the style of clothes won't make much difference. Paul is saying that he is not giving a rule to the churches. He just states what is best in his opinion. We should remember that in all our Christian liberty we are to think of others and of our testimony to others. We should be guided by the principles he has laid down: to glorify God, and not to offend others.

THE LORD'S SUPPER

Now we move to a new topic, and it seems we go from one extreme to the other—from hair and dress to the Lord's Supper. This is probably the most sacred part of our relationship to God. I am confident that the Lord's Supper is something that is greatly misunderstood in our churches. As a result, it is almost blasphemy the way it is observed in some places. Paul is going to say here that God judges us in the way that we observe the Lord's Supper. Actually, among the Corinthians some were sick and some had died because of the way they observed it. They did not discern the body of Christ. I wonder whether we discern the body of Christ today. Most of us observe the method that is used. We note every detail of the ritual, but do we really discern the body of Christ in the Lord's Supper?

The Lord's Supper is the highest expression and the holiest exercise of Christian worship. In Corinth it had dropped to such a low secular level that they were practically blaspheming it. I would have included this section in the "spiritual" division of this epistle except for the fact that Paul is dealing with a very bad situation in Corinth. Therefore, I place it in the "carnal" division of the epistle.

Three of the four Gospels record the institution of the Lord's Supper, and it is repeated in this epistle. It is interesting that nowhere are we commanded to remember the Lord's birthday, but we are requested and commanded that those who are His own should remember His deathday.

Paul attached the utmost importance to the Lord's Supper. In verse 23 he says, "For I have received of the Lord that which also I delivered unto you, That the Lord Jesus the same night in which he was betrayed took bread." Paul received this by direct revelation: "For I delivered unto you first of all that which I also received, how that Christ died for our sins according to the scriptures" (1 Cor. 15:3). Paul received a direct revelation of the gospel and a direct revelation of the Lord's Supper. The Lord gave him special instructions concerning it—remember that Paul was not in the Upper Room at the institution of the Lord's Supper.

I admit that it is rather difficult to see the connection of what Paul says to the Corinthian church with our celebration of the Lord's Supper. There is no exact parallel because the situations are not similar. In that day the Lord's Supper was preceded by a social meal. It was probably celebrated in the homes and celebrated daily. Acts tells us, "And they, continuing daily with one accord in the temple, and breaking bread from house to house, did eat their meat with gladness and singleness of heart, Praising God, and having favour with all the people. And the Lord added to the church daily such as should be saved" [Acts 2:46–47].

Aristides, an Athenian philosopher who lived in the early part of the second century, describes the way the Christians of his day lived: "Every morning and all hours and on the account of the goodness of God towards them they praise and laud Him. . . . And if any righteous person of their number passes away from the world they rejoice and give thanks to God. . . . If a child chance to die in its infancy they praise God mightily, as for one who has passed through this world without sin." That is the statement from one who was not a member of the church but observed it from the outside in the second century.

The church in Corinth followed the procedure of having a meal in connection with the Lord's Supper. After all, the Passover was that kind of celebration in the Upper Room. After our Lord had celebrated the Passover supper, He took bread and broke it. On the dying embers of a fading feast, He did something new. Out of the ashes of that dead feast, He erected a new monument, not of marble or bronze, but of simple elements of food.

Today we have a custom among churches, clubs, fraternities, banks, and insurance companies of getting together and having a meal and a time of fellowship together. A great many folk criticize church banquets, and I have too, when they center only on the physical man. In the early church they had these dinners for fellowship, and they were called an *agape* or "love feast." This was a part of the fellowship of the church, the *koinonia*. In that day the social gathering led right into the Lord's Supper. It was kept separate, but the *agape* always preceded the Eucharist. Later on these feasts were separated, and they are not practiced like that today. We do not have a "love feast" or dinner which precedes the Lord's Supper.

Because of the separation, we do not duplicate the bad situation that prevailed in the Corinthian church. However, there are certain lessons here for us.

> **Now in this that I declare unto you I praise you not, that ye come together not for the better, but for the worse [1 Cor. 11:17].**

The word *declare* is actually a command, and *unto you* in the Authorized Version is in italics, which means it is not in the original text. It should be "Now in this I command, I praise you not, that ye come together not for the better, but for the worse." In other words, they should have come together for a great spiritual blessing, but it didn't amount to that.

> **For first of all, when ye come together in the church, I hear that there be divisions among you; and I partly believe it [1 Cor. 11:18].**

He is not talking about an edifice, a building. He is talking about when the believers come together—that is the true church. Today when we speak of a church, we always identify a building as the church. We think of the Baptist church, the Methodist church, the Presbyterian church, or the independent church down on the corner. The chances are that those buildings are closed and nobody is there. The building is not the church—it is just a building. The church is the people. It is difficult for us to think in a context like that.

When the Corinthian believers came together, the diverse or party spirit that we saw in chapter 1 was carried over into the Lord's Supper. That division was there.

For there must be also heresies among you, that they which are approved may be made manifest among you [1 Cor. 11:19].

This helps to explain the cults and "isms" such as we have in Southern California. Why does God permit them? Let me give you an illustration. Have you ever noticed when a woman is cooking something and there is an accumulation on the top that she skims it off? Well, that is what God does. To tell the truth, I think the churches are filled with unbelievers today. A large percentage of the people in the churches are not saved at all. They are just members of a church. The Lord skims them off. How does He do that? Well, they go off into the cults and the "isms." That is what Paul is saying here: "There must be also heresies among you, that they which are approved may be made manifest among you." Heresy comes along in these cults or "isms," and a lot of people go out of the churches and flock to them. The Lord is skimming them off so that those who are genuine may be revealed.

When ye come together therefore into one place, this is not to eat the Lord's supper [1 Cor. 11:20].

The "this," which is in italics in the Authorized Version, is not in the original. He is saying, "When ye come together into one place, it is not possible to eat the Lord's Supper." It is impossible for them to celebrate the Lord's Supper because of the way that they conducted the feast which preceded it. Under such circumstances they couldn't celebrate the Lord's Supper.

For in eating every one taketh before other his own supper: and one is hungry, and another is drunken [1 Cor. 11:21].

What a comment that is! Some poor fellow would come to the dinner, and he couldn't even bring a covered dish of scalloped potatoes. He was that poor. And he was hungry. Next to him would sit a rich fellow who had fried chicken and ice cream, and he wouldn't pass one bit of food to the poor fellow who was hungry. The fellowship was broken. There could not be fellowship when there was a situation like that.

And then there was something else.

> **What? have ye not houses to eat and to drink in? or despise ye the church of God, and shame them that have not? What shall I say to you? shall I praise you in this? I praise you not [1 Cor. 11:22].**

If they were not going to share in true fellowship, they should have eaten at home. What they were doing was fracturing and rupturing the church. And some were actually getting drunk during this agape love feast. They were in no condition to remember the death of Christ at all. It would be all fuzzy and hazy to them. Paul says again, "Shall I praise you in this? I praise you not."

THE REVELATION TO PAUL

> **For I have received of the Lord that which also I delivered unto you, That the Lord Jesus the same night in which he was betrayed took bread [1 Cor. 11:23].**

Sometimes people say they want to celebrate the Lord's Supper exactly as the Lord did—then they have it at an eleven o'clock morning service. If you want to have it at the time the Lord had it, it must be at night. They went in at night to eat the Passover supper, and it was at that supper that the Lord instituted the Lord's Supper.

It was the very same night in which He was betrayed. At that supper He took bread.

> **And when he had given thanks, he brake it, and said, Take, eat: this is my body, which is broken for you: this do in remembrance of me [1 Cor. 11:24].**

Paul wasn't present in the Upper Room. He got this as a direct revelation from the Lord. It was the night when the forces of hell met to destroy our Savior. I think the simplicity and the sublimity and the sanity of this supper is tremendous.

Notice that it says, "when he had given thanks." He gave thanks that night while the shadow of the Cross hung over the Upper Room. Sin was knocking at the door of the Upper Room, demanding its pound of flesh. And He gave thanks. He gave thanks to God.

Then "he brake it." There has always been a difference of opinion among believers on that. Do you break the bread, or do you serve it as it is? The Roman Catholics break it, the Lutherans do not, and most Protestant churches do not.

In several churches in which I served, I instituted an evening communion because the Lord instituted the Lord's Supper at night. I also tried something else. I asked the one who served the bread to the congregation to take a piece and break it before them. That spoke of the broken body of our Lord.

The breaking of the bread also indicates that this is something that is to be shared. Bengal made this statement: "The very mention of the breaking involves distribution, and rebukes the Corinthian plan of every man his own."

> **After the same manner also he took the cup, when he had supped, saying, This cup is the new testament in my blood: this do ye, as oft as ye drink it, in remembrance of me [1 Cor. 11:25].**

The bread speaks of His broken body; the cup speaks of the new covenant. Have you noticed that it is called the *cup*? (It is also called the fruit of the vine in some instances, but it is never called *wine*). Have I heard that argued! "Should we have fermented or unfermented wine for the Lord's Supper?" That is baby talk to ask questions like that. My friend, we can know it was unfermented. This is Passover, the time of the Feast of Unleavened Bread. Do you think that they had unleavened bread and leavened grape juice (wine is leavened grape juice)? The whole business was unleavened—it had to be at the Passover feast. But the interesting thing is that here Jesus calls it the cup. His body was the cup that held the blood. He was born to die and to shed that blood. Again and again the apostles remind us that we have forgiveness of sins because of the blood, that He has extended mercy to us because of the blood. He did not open the back door of heaven and slip us in under cover of darkness. He brings us in the front door as *sons* because the penalty of sin was paid when the demands of a holy God were met. Let's not forget that, my beloved, in this day when the notion is that God can shut His eyes to sin and do nothing about it. He has done something about it. This is the cup; it holds the blood of the New Covenant.

For as often as ye eat this bread, and drink this cup, ye do shew the Lord's death till he come [1 Cor. 11:26].

Paul here adds something new. In 1 Corinthians he is always opening up a door or raising a shade, letting us see something new. Here it is "till he come." When we observe the Lord's Supper, that table looks in three different directions. (1) It is a commemoration. He repeats, "This do . . . in remembrance of me." This table looks back over nineteen hundred years to His death upon the Cross. He says, "Don't forget that. It is important." That is to the past. (2) This table is a communion (sometimes we call it a communion service). It speaks of the present, of the fact that today there is a *living* Christ, my beloved. (3) It is a commitment. It looks to the future—that He is coming again. This table won't last forever; it is temporary. After the service it is removed, and we may not celebrate it again because we just do it until He comes. It speaks of an absent Lord who is coming back. It looks to the future.

The Lord Jesus Christ took these frail elements—bread and grape juice, which will spoil in a few days, the weakest things in the world—and He raised a monument. It's not of marble, bronze, silver, or gold; it is *bread* and *juice*—that's all. But it speaks of Him, and it tells me that I am responsible for His death.

Wherefore whosoever shall eat this bread, and drink this cup of the Lord, unworthily, shall be guilty of the body and blood of the Lord.

But let a man examine himself, and so let him eat of that bread, and drink of that cup.

For he that eateth and drinketh unworthily, eateth and drinketh damnation to himself, not discerning the Lord's body [1 Cor. 11:27–29].

What does he mean to "discern" the Lord's body? Looking back in church history you will find that the churches had a great problem in determining the meaning of this. What does it mean to discern the Lord's body? The answer of the Roman Catholic church is that transubstantiation takes place, that when the priest officiates at the altar, the bread actually becomes the body of Christ, also that the juice actually becomes the blood of Christ. If this were true, to eat it would be cannibalism. (Thank the Lord, it does not change; it is still bread and juice). But they were wrestling with the problem. How do you discern the Lord's body in this? In the Lutheran church (Martin Luther didn't want to come too far, as he had been a Roman Catholic priest), it is consubstantiation. That is, it is in, by, with, through, and under the bread that you get the body of Christ. It is not the body, but it is the body. You can figure that one out—I can't. Then Zwingli, the Swiss Reformation leader, came all the way. He said it was just a symbol. And the average Protestant today thinks that is all it is, a symbol. I disagree with that explanation as much as I do with the other two. It is more than a symbol.

Follow me now to the Emmaus road, and I think we shall find there recorded in Luke's gospel, chapter 24, what it means to discern Christ's body and His death.

Two of Jesus' disciples, two believers, are walking home after having witnessed the terrible Crucifixion in Jerusalem and the events that followed it. Are they down in the dumps! As they walk along discussing these things, our resurrected Lord joins them and asks what they are talking about that makes them so sad. Thinking Him to be a stranger, they tell Him about Jesus' being condemned to death and crucified and about the report of the women who went to the tomb. "And certain of them which were with us went to the sepulchre, and found it even so as the women had said: but him they saw not. Then he [Christ] said unto them, O fools, and slow of heart to believe all that the prophets have spoken: Ought not Christ to have suffered these things, and to enter into his glory? And beginning at Moses and all the prophets, he expounded unto them in all the scriptures the things concerning himself. And they drew nigh unto the village, whither they went: and he made as though he would have gone further." He acted as if He were going through the town without stopping. "But they constrained him, saying, Abide with us: for it is toward evening, and the day is far spent." It was dangerous to walk those highways at night.

"And he went in to tarry with them. And it came to pass, as he sat at meat with them. . . ." A few days before He had eaten the Passover with His own, now these are two other disciples, and here is the first time after His resurrection He is observing the Lord's Supper. "And it came to pass, as he sat at meat with them, he took bread, and blessed it, and brake, and gave to them." Wasn't that wonderful to have Him present for the meal! In the meal He takes the bread, He breaks it, He blesses it, He gives it to them. "And their eyes were opened, and they knew him; and he vanished out of their sight. And they said one to another, Did not our heart burn within us . . . ?" (Luke 24:24–32). He had a meal with them. Then what did He do? He *revealed* Himself. That was the Lord's Supper.

Oh, friend, when you observe the Lord's Supper, He is present. Yes, He is! This is not just a symbol. It means you must discern the body of Christ. You have bread in your mouth, but you have Christ in your heart. May God help us to so come to the table that Jesus Christ will be a *reality* to us. God forgive us for making it a dead, formal ritual!

For this cause many are weak and sickly among you, and many sleep [1 Cor. 11:30].

They suffered sickness and death. Why? Because they had partici-
pated in the Lord's Supper unworthily—that is, in an unworthy manner.

> **For if we would judge ourselves, we should not be
> judged.**
>
> **But when we are judged, we are chastened of the Lord,
> that we should not be condemned with the world [1 Cor.
> 11:31–32].**

This is talking about believers. We can judge ourselves when we are
wrong. If we don't, He will judge us. When we are judged of the Lord,
we are chastened so that we shall not be condemned with the world.
He is going to judge the world in the future. Therefore He has to deal
with His own now.

> **Wherefore, my brethren, when ye come together to eat,
> tarry one for another.**
>
> **And if any man hunger, let him eat at home; that ye
> come not together unto condemnation. And the rest will
> I set in order when I come [1 Cor. 11:33–34].**

There were other things wrong in the Corinthian church, but Paul is
not going to write about them now. He says that he will straighten out
those things when he gets there.

CHAPTER 12

THEME: Endowment of gifts

The first section of 1 Corinthians had to do with carnalities, as we have seen. Chapter 12 begins a new section which deals with spiritualities. And the first three chapters concern spiritual gifts: chapter 12, the *endowment* of gifts; chapter 13, the *energy* of gifts; chapter 14, the *exercise* of gifts.

GIFTS ARE GIVEN TO MAINTAIN UNITY IN DIVERSITY

Now concerning spiritual gifts, brethren, I would not have you ignorant [1 Cor. 12:1].

Notice that in the text of your Bible the word *gifts* is in italics, which means that that word is not in the original. It was added for the sake of clarity; but, very frankly, I don't think adding the word clarified anything. Actually, it has added confusion. In *The Revised Standard Version* it is spiritual gifts; in *The New English Bible* it is gifts of the Spirit; in *The Berkeley Translation* it is spiritual endowments. *The Scofield Reference Bible* has a good footnote about this.

The Greek word is *pneumatika*, which literally means "spiritualities." It is in contrast to carnalities. One does not need to add the word "gifts." Back in the third chapter Paul was discussing the divisions among the Corinthian believers, and he wrote, "And I, brethren, could not speak unto you as unto spiritual, but as unto carnal, even as unto babes in Christ" (1 Cor. 3:1). That first section is about carnalities because their questions were about carnalities and the things that carnal Christians would be interested in. The carnalities had to do with their divisions, their wrangling about different leaders, about adultery, about going to court against a brother, the sex problem, women's dress and men's haircuts, the love feast, gluttony and drunkenness at the Lord's Supper. That is all carnality, and we can find the same things in the church today. The section on carnalities was corrective.

Now we come to the section on spiritualities, and this is constructive. Paul was glad to change the subject; I think he heaved a sigh of relief when he got here to chapter 12. He was willing to discuss the other problems with them, but he really wanted to talk to them about the spiritualities.

The modern church needs to change the same old subjects which are discussed. In a very sophisticated manner Christian educators say that we should tell our young people about sex. Friend, we had better tell them about spiritual things. There are so many programs in the churches that the young people never get anywhere near the Bible. They have conferences on whatever carnality is the popular issue or the fad for the moment. All of that is a sign of carnality.

In this section Paul will touch on three subjects: the unifying Spirit, the law of love, and the triumph the believer has in the Resurrection. The gifts of the Spirit just happen to be one of the spiritualities, by the way.

Ye know that ye were Gentiles, carried away unto these dumb idols, even as ye were led [1 Cor. 12:2].

The idols were voiceless, dumb idols. Remember that previously Paul said the idols are "nothings." That is why the meat offered to the idols was not contaminated. The idols were nothing. Unfortunately, everyone doesn't quite understand that. Back in Psalm 115:5 the psalmist says, "They have mouths, but they speak not: eyes have they, but they see not." This is what Habakkuk wrote: "What profiteth the graven image that the maker thereof hath graven it; the molten image, and a teacher of lies, that the maker of his work trusteth therein, to make dumb idols?" (Hab. 2:18).

The very interesting thing is that he is going to talk about the gifts that the living God gives to believers. So first he reminds them how they formerly were carried away unto these dumb idols.

> Wherefore I give you to understand, that no man speaking by the Spirit of God calleth Jesus accursed: and that no man can say that Jesus is the Lord, but by the Holy Ghost [1 Cor. 12:3].

Here is a great truth, an absolute verity of the Christian life: the lordship of Jesus Christ. "No man speaking by the Spirit of God calleth Jesus accursed." You cannot belittle Jesus Christ by the Spirit of God. It won't work. Also, "no man can say that Jesus is the Lord, but by the Holy [Spirit] Ghost." Oh, of course we can pronounce the word Lord. But remember what the Lord Jesus said: "Not every one that saith unto me, Lord, Lord, shall enter into the kingdom of heaven; but he that doeth the will of my Father which is in heaven. Many will say to me in that day, Lord, Lord, have we not prophesied in thy name? and in thy name have cast out devils? and in thy name done many wonderful works? And then will I profess unto them, I never knew you: depart from me, ye that work iniquity" (Matt. 7:21–23). Why will that be? Because their profession is on the surface. The Lord Jesus was not their Lord.

Making Jesus Lord is a conviction of the soul. What is the central truth of the Christian faith? There are those who say it is the Cross of Christ, but I rather disagree with that. Although we come to the Cross to be saved, we do not stay at the Cross. We become united to the living Christ. That is the thing which is all important.

Listen to the way Simon Peter concluded his message on the Day of Pentecost: "Therefore let all the house of Israel know assuredly, that God hath made that same Jesus, whom ye have crucified, both Lord and Christ" (Acts 2:36). He is the Lord. He is sovereign. His sovereignty is the important thing in the Christian life.

The Holy Spirit commands the soul's obedience and allegiance to Jesus. The true church is made up of those who have gathered around that truth as interpreted by the Holy Spirit. The Holy Spirit interprets the lordship of Jesus to my life. Remember the great question which Jesus asked, ". . . whom say ye that I am?" (Matt. 16:15). Jesus is still asking that same question. You may be of any occupation, any color, any status in life—whoever you are, wherever you are, however you are—Jesus asks you, "Whom say ye that I am?" He asked His disciples that question, and Simon Peter spoke for the group. He said, "... Thou art the Christ, the Son of the living God" (Matt. 16:16). He is the Anointed One. He is the King. He is the Lord. No man is fit to serve Christ's church unless he has been mastered by Jesus Christ. We have seen that earlier in this epistle. Now Paul emphasizes that again.

The *unifying* work of the Holy Spirit today is to reveal the lordship of Jesus to all believers. Within this unity there is *diversity* of gifts.

Now there are diversities of gifts, but the same Spirit [1 Cor. 12:4].

There is a distribution of gifts. In order to have the unity, He gives different gifts to different individuals. The Greek word for "gifts" is *charisma*. Some people try to make this word apply to tongues, and they speak of the charismatic movement. This reveals their ignorance, as the word refers to *all* the gifts which the Holy Spirit gives to the believers in the church.

And there are differences of administrations, but the same Lord [1 Cor. 12:5].

That is, there are diversities of ministrations, but the same Lord—the Lord Jesus Christ. It doesn't make any difference which gift you may have. It is the Lord Jesus who is using that gift, and He is using it for His glory.

And there are diversities of operations, but it is the same God which worketh all in all [1 Cor. 12:6].

There are diversities of operations—that is, of the energy. But it is the same God who works in all, and He is the One who works in the believer.

This reminds us that there is but one God—but He is a Trinity. The Trinity works together; there is a unity. But there is a diversity in unity. Notice this: The Holy Spirit bestows the gifts; the Lord Jesus

Christ administers the gifts—they are under His direction; the Father God supplies the power, and He energizes the gifts. All of this is for the one purpose of exalting and glorifying the lordship of Jesus Christ.

But the manifestation of the Spirit is given to every man to profit withal [1 Cor. 12:7].

First of all, let's define a *gift*. What is a gift of the Spirit? It is a capacity for service. It is a function. This is Dr. Lewis Sperry Chafer's definition: "A gift in the spiritual sense means the Holy Spirit doing a particular service through the believer and using the believer to do it." To this I would like to add that it must be done in the power of the Spirit of God. To make this personal: I am nothing, I have nothing, I am of no use to God or man. That is not a pious platitude; it is a fact. But He gave me a gift, and I'm to exercise that gift. That is, I believe, the only way the Spirit of God will manifest Himself in my life.

"The manifestation of the Spirit is given to every man to profit withal." "Manifestation of the Spirit"—that is what a gift is. A gift is the manifestation of the Spirit.

This does not necessarily mean the exercise of a natural gift. For example, a woman has a gift of singing. She has a marvelous voice. But if she does not sing in the power of the Holy Spirit, God can't use it—and He *doesn't* use it. This is the reason that music in the average contemporary church has sunk to such a low level. Musicians think that all they need is talent and training. They think if they have that, they have it made, and the Lord can't get along without them. The fact of the matter is that He can get along *better* without them. I have been in many, many places across the country and have ministered in many pulpits. I have learned much through the years, and I can tell when a musician is adding to the service or detracting from it. I have had the experience of hearing a solo sung immediately before the message that absolutely ruined the message before I even stood to my feet. I have felt like getting up, pronouncing the benediction, and going home. Now let me make it very clear that I believe the Holy Spirit can use the natural ability of a believer if the believer will let Him do it. But natural talent alone is nothing unless it is under the control of the Holy Spirit.

There are those who have no particular natural talent. They say that since they can't sing in the choir or teach in the Sunday school, there is nothing for them to do but to sit in the pew. That is one of the most tragic mistakes made in the church.

This verse tells us that every believer has a gift. Every believer! "But the manifestation of the Spirit is given to every man to profit withal."

The word for "man" in the Greek is *anthropōs*, which is a generic term and actually means man or woman, boy or girl. It doesn't make any difference who you are. If you are a child of God, you have a gift. You have been put into the body of believers as a member of the body, and you are to function as a member of the body of Christ.

"The manifestation of the Spirit is given to every man to profit withal." What is the purpose of the gift? It is to build up the church, the body of believers. It is not to be exercised selfishly, but is to give spiritual help to other believers.

For to one is given by the Spirit the word of wisdom; to another the word of knowledge by the same Spirit [1 Cor. 12:8].

"Wisdom" means insight into truth. I do not think everyone can come to an understanding of the Bible, which is the reason we need teachers, and the Spirit of God has given us teachers. "Wisdom" is insight into the truth of the Word of God. "Knowledge" means to investigate or to dig into the truth. Many people simply do not have the time to dig into the Word of God, to dig out the nuggets. One man who supports our radio program very generously says, "I'm just paying for the nuggets that you deliver to me." As a businessman and executive he does not have hours and hours to study. I don't think God is asking him to do that. He supports the program, and I do the digging for him. I think that is my gift. So he and I are working together as partners, each exercising his own gift. This is very practical.

To another faith by the same Spirit; to another the gifts of healing by the same Spirit [1 Cor. 12:9].

Faith, we are told in the Scriptures, is the substance of things hoped for. That is a gift. Some people have the gift of faith.

I have a combination of Scottish and German blood in me. When you get that combination, it's bad. I have pessimist blood in me, and I look at everything from that point of view. In every church in which I served, God gave me several people who had the gift of faith. Many a time an officer has come and put his arm around my shoulder and said, "Look, preacher, this thing is going to come through just right." And you know, it did. He had the faith; I didn't. Faith is a gift of the Spirit.

"To another the gifts of healing by the same Spirit." That means that the sick were healed by the laying on of hands. I believe this was a gift given to the apostles and to men in the early church. I don't think that gift is needed today. We should take our case directly to the Great Physician. We don't need to go through a man or woman down here and ask them to pray for us or lay their hands on us. Take your case directly to Him.

Remember that the centurion came to Jesus and asked Him to heal his servant. He didn't ask Jesus to lay hands on his servant. He simply asked Jesus to say the word and his servant would be healed. He had faith, such faith that Jesus marveled at him and said, ". . . I say unto you, I have not found so great faith, no, not in Israel" (Luke 7:9). So take your case directly to the Great Physician. It reveals a lack of faith in Him to go to a so-called healer.

I believe that the Holy Spirit gives certain gifts that are peculiar for specific ages. No one today has the same gift that Martin Luther had in his day. I think the Spirit of God gives gifts to the body of Christ so that it might function in the age in which it finds itself in order that the whole body might profit from it.

To another the working of miracles; to another prophecy; to another discerning of spirits; to another divers

kinds of tongues; to another the interpretation of tongues [1 Cor. 12:10].

"The working of miracles" is to do supernatural things. There were miracles in the apostolic age, but today we are seeing greater things. When Jesus was here and He spoke a word to a person—like the woman at the well or to Nicodemus—and that person was converted, I don't marvel at that. But when I speak the Word or you speak the Word and somebody is saved, that is a greater work.

To "prophesy" means to declare the will of Christ. That is, to prophesy is to preach the Word of God. We need people today who are willing to do that. We need people who will speak the Word of God and then trust God to use that Word through His Spirit.

The "discerning of spirits" means the ability to distinguish between the false and the true. I am convinced that I do not have that gift at all. I have been deceived probably more than any preacher ever has been deceived. I have trusted men—certain preachers and certain church officers—and thought they were genuine; yet they have let me down horribly. I have been deceived by liars and dishonest folk whom I thought to be wonderful people. On the other hand, you find some people who have discerning of spirits. My wife has been a great help to me in this connection. She tells me, "Now you be careful there, watch out for that individual," or "I think this one is a very wonderful person." She is generally right, and I am generally wrong. She has the discerning of spirits.

Another gift is "kinds of tongues" (the word *divers* is not in the original). Are these unknown tongues? No, you do not find unknown tongues in Scripture. These are known languages. There are still many, many languages into which the Bible has not been translated. Instead of wasting time trying to invent an unknown language, let's get the gospel translated into these known languages that don't have it yet. Some folk have the gift of translating.

But all these worketh that one and the selfsame Spirit, dividing to every man severally as he will [1 Cor. 12:11].

The Holy Spirit is sovereign in all this. However, we do have the right to pray for the best gifts, which is what Paul is going to tell these Corinthians. They were carnal Christians, living on a very low spiritual level. They were fascinated by the tongues movement. That is why Paul is discussing it in this epistle. He was trying to correct the things that were wrong in the Corinthian church, and there were many things wrong. He is showing them that there are many gifts and that the Holy Spirit distributes to each one individually as *He* wills.

MEMBERS OF THE HUMAN BODY COMPARED TO GIFTS OF THE HOLY SPIRIT

For as the body is one, and hath many members, and all the members of that one body, being many, are one body: so also is Christ [1 Cor. 12:12].

In the consideration of this passage let us drop down to include two other verses: "But now are they many members, yet but one body" (v. 20) and "Now ye are the body of Christ, and members in particular" (v. 27). Paul is using a comparison to the human body. As one body has many members performing different functions, so the members of the church need to perform different functions. The human body has many members, hundreds, even thousands of members. In the church, the body of Christ, there are many gifts, hundreds, probably thousands of gifts.

On a hunting trip I stepped off a cliff and hurt my foot. When I went to the doctor, I asked him how many bones were in the foot. He told me there were twenty-seven. I said, "I think I hurt all twenty-seven of them!" "No," he said, "you hurt only one." Now I tell you, I may have hurt only one of them, but my whole foot was painful. When one member suffers, they all suffer.

The body is composed of many members. There are the bones and muscles, the glands and the organs, the nerves and the blood vessels. On one occasion, after I had spoken at a baccalaureate service in a prep school in Atlanta, Georgia, I went to a doctor's home for dinner. He asked me if I knew which was the most important part of my body while I had been speaking. I guessed it was my tongue. "No," he said, "the most important part of your body today was a member that no one was conscious of. It was your big toe. If you didn't have a couple of big toes, you wouldn't have been able to stand up there at all."

I have thought a great deal about that. Suppose when I would go somewhere to preach, my big toe would rebel and say, "Look here, I refuse to go. I've been going with you for years and you have never called attention to me. People see your lips and tongue and your face, but they don't ever see me. Why don't you ever take off your shoe and sock and let them get a look at me sometime?" Well, now, I don't think folk would be interested in seeing my big toe—it is not very attractive. In fact, it is unattractive, yet it is an important part of my body.

There are many members in the body of Christ. Some of them we don't ever see. Some of the most important members in churches where I have served have been men and women whom the church knew nothing about. They weren't the officers or the Sunday school teachers or the soloist or the preacher. They were quiet, unobtrusive folk who prayed and who exercised their gift of faith.

Now how does a person get into this body of believers?

For by one Spirit are we all baptized into one body, whether we be Jews or Gentiles, whether we be bond or free; and have been all made to drink into one Spirit [1 Cor. 12:13].

This is the baptism of the Holy Spirit. It is the Holy Spirit who puts us into the body of believers and who gives a gift to each particular member. We are to function in that body, and we are to use that gift. It may be that we are the "big toes" with an unseen but important ministry. We each have a gift, and we are each to function.

For the body is not one member, but many.

If the foot shall say, Because I am not the hand, I am not of the body; is it therefore not of the body?

> And if the ear shall say, Because I am not the eye, I am
> not of the body; is it therefore not of the body?
>
> If the whole body were an eye, where were the hearing?
> If the whole were hearing, where were the smelling?
> [1 Cor. 12:14–17].

Suppose there would be a return of the gift of tongues such as there was in the apostolic times. It still would be true that not everyone would speak in tongues. The analogy is to our bodies. Our bodies are not all tongue. (I have met a few people who seemed to be all tongue, but they are exceptions!) The Holy Spirit is not going to give the same gift to every person. Like the human body, there need to be eyes and ears and feet and hands. Different people are given different gifts by the Spirit of God so that the body of Christ can function in all its necessary capacities.

> But now hath God set the members every one of them in
> the body, as it hath pleased him [1 Cor. 12:18].

God is the One who sovereignly gives the gifts, and He gives them as it pleases Him. He is the One to be pleased, you see. These gifts are in the body so that the body can function.

A man in one of my congregations had an unusual gift. He was not an usher, but he would stand in the back of the church and if there was any kind of disruption or commotion in the service, he would take care of it. If a baby was crying in the church, one of the ushers might ask the mother to leave and antagonize her by doing so. But this man had a gift. He would go to the mother and play with the baby a few minutes and then say, "By the way, we have a nursery here. Would you like me to take the baby down there or show you where the nursery is?" The mothers always responded. He just had a way of handling people. As I told him, he had a rare gift and one that is needed in the church.

You may be surprised that something like that is a gift. Of course, it is a gift, and so is cooking or baking or sewing.

We can get some idea about gifts from incidents in the Bible. Ananias and Sapphira had gifts, but they had not submitted to the lordship of Jesus Christ, and their gifts were not functioning for the Lord. So they fell down dead before Simon Peter. They couldn't exist in the early church. They had gifts, but they were not exercising them as they should.

There was a woman by the name of Dorcas who had a gift of sewing, and she used that gift under the lordship of Christ. She exercised it in the will of God. When she died, Simon Peter went to Joppa and the widows had a regular fashion show as they showed Peter the dresses that Dorcas had made. The reason they wore them was that these were all that those poor women had to wear. Dorcas and her gift were important in the early church, so much so that Peter raised her from the dead. She had a gift that was still needed.

Simon Peter had a gift. He was the great preacher on the Day of Pentecost. God used him mightily. When God no longer needed his gift, he died—he was not raised from the dead.

My friend, the Spirit of God is sovereign in all this. He is the One who determines what is important and what is not important. If God has called you to bake a cake or to sew a dress, then do it. That is a gift. The Holy Spirit wants us to use our gifts and to bring them under the lordship of Jesus Christ.

And if they were all one member, where were the body?

But now are they many members, yet but one body.

And the eye cannot say unto the hand, I have no need of thee: nor again the head to the feet, I have no need of you.

Nay, much more those members of the body, which seem to be more feeble, are necessary [1 Cor. 12:19–22].

You and I need each other, and the Lord wants to use all of us.

And those members of the body, which we think to be less honourable, upon these we bestow more abundant

honour; and our uncomely parts have more abundant comeliness.

For our comely parts have no need: but God hath tempered the body together, having given more abundant honour to that part which lacked:

That there should be no schism in the body; but that the members should have the same care one for another [1 Cor. 12:23-25].

You have seen some little, underdeveloped boy taking exercises and lifting weights. He is trying to develop some muscles and trying to develop some strength. Just so, God pays attention to the body of believers so that the small gifts are developed. I think there are many gifts in the church which need to be developed today.

Perhaps you feel that you are not doing anything for the Lord. One of the most thrilling things in the world, especially if you are a young person, is to find out what God wants you to do and where He wants you to go. What a thrill, what an experience, what an adventure to find out what gift God has given you!

Paul goes on to say that this should all be done so that there is no schism in the body. The members should all have the same care one for another.

And whether one member suffer, all the members suffer with it; or one member be honoured, all the members rejoice with it [1 Cor. 12:26].

My friend, there is no place for jealousy in the church—we all are members of the same body. If one is honored, we all receive that honor. And when one member is suffering, we all suffer with him.

Now ye are the body of Christ, and members in particular.

And God hath set some in the church, first apostles, secondarily prophets, thirdly teachers, after that mira-

cles, then gifts of healings, helps, governments, diversities of tongues [1 Cor. 12:27-28].

What about the gift of "helps"? Oh, what a wonderful gift that is! If you have it, I hope you are exercising it.

Are all apostles? are all prophets? are all teachers? are all workers of miracles?

Have all the gifts of healing? do all speak with tongues? do all interpret? [1 Cor. 12:29-30].

Some of these gifts have disappeared. They are not in the church because they are not needed in the church today. There are no longer apostles in the church, nor are there prophets—in the sense of being able to foretell future events.

Paul also makes it very clear that all people do not have all the gifts. Are all apostles? The obvious answer is, "No." Do all work miracles, or do all have the gift of healing, or do all speak with tongues? The answer is, "No, they do not."

But covet earnestly the best gifts: and yet shew I unto you a more excellent way [1 Cor. 12:31].

Although the Holy Spirit is sovereign in bestowing gifts, we have the right to ask God for the gift we want. He says we are to "covet earnestly the best gifts."

Not having been brought up in a Christian home, I had no Christian training at all. When I went away to seminary, I didn't even know the books of the Bible. I had graduated from a college where the emphasis was placed on the intellectual and the philosophical, and I was trying to be that kind of preacher. Then I heard Dr. Harry Ironside speak. He explained Scripture in a simple manner. And I heard him make the statement, "Put cookies on the bottom shelf so the kiddies can get them." And I remembered that my Lord had said, "Feed my sheep" (see John 21:16). He hadn't said, "Feed my giraffes." So I went to God and prayed, "Lord, I want to be *that* kind of preacher."

Later, I substituted for Dr. Ironside at Dallas Theological Seminary, and when he passed on, the seminary's president, Dr. Lewis Sperry Chafer, called me on the phone. He asked, "Would you take Dr. Ironside's lectures here at the seminary?" I could hardly answer him clearly, and I almost rudely hung up the phone. I dropped to my knees, and I confess that I wept as I thanked God. I said, "Lord I prayed that You would let me teach like Dr. Ironside, and You have answered my prayer!" I coveted earnestly the best gift, and He answered my prayer. Although I am no Dr. Ironside, how I thrill today at the experience and the privilege of teaching the Word of God!

My friend, you have the right to ask God for the *best* gift. Several folk have written this to me: "I certainly hope you receive the baptism of the Holy Spirit." Well, for your information, I have received it, not as an experience or something I received after I was saved, but the Holy Spirit has put me into this body of believers, which is the *baptism* of the Holy Spirit. Also these folk say, "We hope that you will speak in tongues." Well, my prayer is that I can speak in the English language a little better. Why? For the simple reason that the gift God gives us is for the profit—the wealth of the church. Regardless of the gift God gives to you, the purpose of it is to be helpful to other believers, other members of the body.

CHAPTER 13

THEME: Love—the energy of the gifts

This chapter is properly called the *love* chapter of the Bible. Many men have attempted to give an exposition of it. Frankly, I have preached on it only once or twice in my ministry. Although I have taught it whenever I have come to it in a program of going through the Bible on radio or at any of the churches I have served, candidly, it is a passage that passes beyond my comprehension and capability. In 1884 Henry Drummond wrote a very brilliant essay entitled, *The Greatest Thing in the World*. It was put into my hands very early in my Christian life. It is a great little book on this thirteenth chapter.

The word *charity*, which is used throughout this chapter, should be *love*. The Vulgate, which is the Latin translation, and Wycliffe's English translation used the word *charity*, and this word was carried over into the King James Version. The Greek word is *agape*, which is properly translated *love*.

You will not find a definition of love in this chapter. Sometimes definitions are destructive. To try to define love would actually be a very serious violation of this chapter. When you try to define a rose, you can read the description of a rose that botany gives you, but that definition doesn't picture a rose like I know a rose to be. Or have you ever had anyone describe a sunset for you? I remember one evening at the Island of Saint Thomas in the Virgin Islands standing on the deck of a little boat and seeing the moon come up. It was such a thrill that it made the goose pimples come up all over me. I wish I could picture it for you, but I cannot. This chapter gives to us a *display* of love, not a definition.

There are three words in the Greek which are all translated by our one word *love*. There is the word *eros*. That is the word for passion, the word used for lust. It is used of Aphrodite and Eros, or Venus and Cupid as we more commonly know them. Sex would be our word for it today. This word does not occur in the New Testament at all.

Then there is the word *phileō*, which means "affection." We find that root in our words *Philadelphia* and *philanthropist*. It means a love of man, a love of a brother. It means human love at its highest, a noble love.

The word *agapaō* is the highest word for love in the New Testament and means "divine love." It is more than love in the emotion; it is love in the will. It is love that chooses its object. It is a definition of God, for God is love.

Now I am going to give you an outline of the chapter. Again, this seems like a violation of the chapter, but the mechanics will help us understand it.

The preeminence of love—its value (vv. 1–3)
The prerogative of love—its virtue (vv. 4–7)
The permanence of love—its victory (vv. 8–13)

Remember how this chapter follows the thought in chapter 12, which was the *endowment* of gifts. Chapter 13 tells of the *energy* of the gifts. All gifts of the Spirit are to be exercised in love.

PREEMINENCE OF LOVE—ITS VALUE

Though I speak with the tongues of men and of angels, and have not charity, I am become as sounding brass, or a tinkling cymbal [1 Cor. 13:1].

I am sure the tongues of angels means eloquence. I have never heard an angel speak, but I think Paul had heard them.

The most marvelous eloquence without love is nothing in the world but a noisy bell. Dr. Scroggie says it like this: "Language without love is noise without melody." McGee says it like this: "Chatter without charity is sound without soul." You can sing like a seraph, but without love it is nothing but the hiss of hell. Love gives meaning and depth and reality, and it makes eloquence meaningful.

And though I have the gift of prophecy, and understand all mysteries, and all knowledge; and though I have all

faith, so that I could remove mountains, and have not charity, I am nothing [1 Cor. 13:2].

The first verse was speaking of love as it comes from the heart. This is from the mind, love as an act of the intellect. Knowledge alone is not sufficient. Love must be added to that knowledge. Understanding alone is not enough. Love must be added to that understanding. I feel this is the sad plight of Bible-believing churches in our day. There is a knowledge of the Bible and an understanding of the truths of the Bible but a lack of love. How terrible to find churches filled with gossip, bitterness, and hatred! Along with knowledge there must be love.

And though I bestow all my goods to feed the poor, and though I give my body to be burned, and have not charity, it profiteth me nothing [1 Cor. 13:3].

This love is an act of the will. Love involves the heart (v. 1), the mind (v. 2), and the will (v. 3). Love is a fruit of the Holy Spirit. Although we are to covet earnestly the best gifts, they are to be exercised in love—and only the Spirit of God can do that.

Look at it this way: Write down a string of zeros—eloquence alone is zero, prophecy alone is zero, knowledge alone is zero, faith alone is zero, sacrifice alone is zero, martyrdom alone is zero. Six zeros still add up to nothing. But you put the numeral 1 to the left of that string of zeros, and every zero amounts to something. And, friend, love is the thing that needs to be added to every gift of the Spirit. Without love your gift is worthless.

PREROGATIVE OF LOVE—ITS VIRTUE

Charity suffereth long, and is kind; charity envieth not; charity vaunteth not itself, is not puffed up [1 Cor. 13:4].

"Love suffers long," which means it is patient and kind. Love is impossible without kindness. Love without kindness is like springtime without flowers, like fire without heat. Remember how Paul admonished, "And be ye kind one to another, tenderhearted, forgiving one another, even as God for Christ's sake hath forgiven you" (Eph. 4:32). This is the positive side. Now notice the negative side.

"Love envieth not." Love does not envy, which means that love is content with its lot. We all know that life is filled with inequality. Some men are rich, and I hear Christians say, "Why did God bless that man with so much wealth and not give me some?" Love recognizes that there are inequalities, and love is satisfied with its lot. Remember that the very first murder, when Cain slew Abel, was prompted by envy.

We do well to ponder the example of John the Baptist who showed no envy when the ministry of Jesus was growing in popularity with the people. John said, "He must increase, but I must decrease" (John 3:30). When we consider that we each have a different lot in life and each have a different ministry for the Lord, we should consider the words of our Lord Himself when He talked to Peter: ". . . If I will that he tarry till I come, what is that to thee? follow thou me" (John 21:22). Bacon said that envy "is a vile affection and it's most depraved of any thing."

An example of a man who loved another man without envy is Jonathan. Although he was the crown prince, he did not envy David even though he knew that David would occupy the throne in his stead.

"Love vaunteth not itself." Moffitt translates this "makes no parade." It is not boastful or ostentatious. You know, there is a vulgarity about boasting.

A young preacher stood up in a conference in Tennessee and said, "I want you to know that I'm not a trained minister. I am an ignorant minister, and I'm proud of it." The bishop answered him, "I can see you have a lot to be proud of, and, young man, it is dangerous to boast even about ignorance."

Love is "not puffed up." That means it does not travel on air—it is not inflated. You know what it is like to be traveling on a tire filled with air, then suddenly have a flat tire. There is many a flat tire even among Christians because there are so many who are puffed up. When the air is gone, there is nothing there!

Doth not behave itself unseemly, seeketh not her own, is not easily provoked, thinketh no evil [1 Cor. 13:5].

Love does not behave itself unseemly; that is, it doesn't act peculiar. It is true that in 1 Peter the believers are called a peculiar people, but they shouldn't act peculiar. It literally means a people for His possession. We are to exercise courtesy. We are not to be rude. We are not to act like strange people. We ought to be polite. Unfortunately, there is so much today that can be called unlovely religion. But love does not behave itself unseemly.

Love "seeketh not her own." Love inquires into the motives for action; that is, it asks, "Why am I doing this?" Since I have been retired, I have examined my own heart as I never did before. I have searched out my own motives. Am I doing it out of love for Christ? That is so important. Love is the secret of service.

Love "is not easily provoked." It doesn't have a bad temper. Being provoked is the vice of the virtuous. I'm afraid it is the vice of many of us.

Love "thinketh no evil." How sad it is to see people thrive on gossip. There are Christians who ladle up dirt. They are suggestive in what they have to say.

Rejoiceth not in iniquity, but rejoiceth in the truth [1 Cor. 13:6].

Love does not rejoice in iniquity, but love rejoices in the truth. What brings joy to your heart? Bad or good? Which is it? If you hear something bad about someone who is your enemy or whom you do not like, do you rejoice? Or does it make you sad to see your enemy suffer?

Beareth all things, believeth all things, hopeth all things, endureth all things [1 Cor. 13:7].

Love bears all things. "Bears" has the thought of protection. Love puts up an umbrella for others.

Love "believeth all things." That does not mean that love is foolishly credulous. It does mean that love does not regard people with suspicion.

Love "hopeth all things." Oh, the optimism of love!

It "endureth all things." Love remains strong through testing.

We learn from all this that love is an abstract noun, but it is not to remain abstract. It is to be translated into life and action. It is to express itself in action through patience, through kindness, without envy, without boastfulness.

PERMANENCE OF LOVE—ITS VICTORY

Charity never faileth; but whether there be prophecies, they shall fail; whether there be tongues, they shall cease; whether there be knowledge, it shall vanish away [1 Cor. 13:8].

Love never fails. That is why at the end of the chapter it says, "Now abideth faith, hope, charity, these three; but the greatest of these is charity." Love abides. It is permanent.

Elizabeth Barrett Browning wrote a poem entitled "I Loved Once," in which she writes, "They never loved who dreamed that they loved once," and "Love looks beyond the bounds of time and space, Love takes eternity in its embrace." Love is deathless. It is never defeated, never disillusioned, never disappointed. Love that is a passion burns like a straw stack and is soon consumed. That is the reason there are so many divorces today. It was not the kind of love that holds two hearts together. Love is eternal. It is permanent. God's love is that kind of love. How wonderful that is! His love looks beyond the bounds of time and space and takes eternity in its embrace. Christ never ceased loving. You can't do anything to keep Him from loving. No sinner has committed an unpardonable sin. You may be in the state of unbelief, but He still loves you. You may have committed ever so great a sin, but He still loves you. You cannot keep Him from loving you. You can put up an umbrella to keep yourself out of the rain, but you cannot stop the rain from falling. Neither can you stop God from loving you—regardless of the umbrella of sin or unbelief that you are under.

It is so wrong to tell children that God won't love them. I used to be in a Sunday school class of little fellows. They were a bunch of mean brats—I was the only good boy in the class! The teacher would say to us, "God won't love you boys if you keep acting that way." I used to think, *God surely can't love me very much*. But He *did* in spite of my meanness. How wonderful it is to know that God loves us!

Prophecies shall fail—that is, they will be fulfilled. They will then be history, not prophecy. Tongues are going to stop. Knowledge will vanish away. For example, the science that I learned in college is already out of date. The science of today will be replaced by the science of tomorrow. Knowledge is progressive. It vanishes away.

> **For we know in part, and we prophesy in part.**
>
> **But when that which is perfect is come, then that which is in part shall be done away [1 Cor. 13:9–10].**

Paul says this:

> **When I was a child, I spake as a child, I understood as a child, I thought as a child: but when I became a man, I put away childish things.**
>
> **For now we see through a glass, darkly; but then face to face: now I know in part; but then shall I know even as also I am known [1 Cor. 13:11–12].**

A great many people ask, "Will I know my loved ones in heaven?" You surely will. What is the scriptural proof? "Now we see through a glass, darkly." You have never seen me. It is possible you may think you have seen me, but what you saw was a suit of clothes with a head and two hands sticking out of it. You didn't really see me. And I have never really seen you because we just see through a glass, darkly, but then face to face. Now I know only in part, but then I shall know even as also I am known. Someone asked G. Campbell Morgan, "Do you think we will know our loved ones in heaven?" Dr. Morgan in his truly British manner answered, "I do not expect to be a bigger fool in heaven than I am here, and I know my loved ones here."

And now abideth faith, hope, charity, these three; but the greatest of these is charity [1 Cor. 13:13].

The object of our faith will be fulfilled. All our hopes will be realized. There will be nothing left to hope for; so hope will disappear. There will be no need for faith. However, love is going to abide. The greatest of these is love. Faith, hope, and love are the high words of the Christian vocabulary.

In this chapter Paul is not describing an abstract term—love. He is writing a biography of Jesus Christ. Of Him it was written, ". . . having loved his own which were in the world, he loved them unto the end" (John 13:1). The love of Jesus is an eternal love. My friend, Jesus Christ will never cease loving you.

CHAPTER 14

THEME: Exercise of gifts

W e are in the section of the epistle concerning spiritual gifts. In chapter 12 we saw the endowment of gifts. Gifts were given to maintain the unity of the church in a diversity. Each member has a separate gift; yet all are to function together as the body functions with its many members. The eye cannot do what the ear does, and the ear cannot do what the eye does. Each must function in its own way.

We are put into the body of Christ by the Holy Spirit, and we are placed there to exercise a gift. Paul tells us at the end of chapter 12 that we should covet earnestly the best gifts, and yet he will show us a more excellent way. That way is by love. The entire chapter 13 is on the subject of love. He concludes by saying that the greatest of these is love, and he continues by saying that we are to follow after love.

GIFT OF PROPHECY IS SUPERIOR
TO GIFT OF TONGUES

P aul now follows right on and says that we should follow after love, but we should desire spiritualities.

Follow after charity, and desire spiritual gifts, but rather that ye may prophesy [1 Cor. 14:1].

We should desire spiritual gifts—I think it would be unusual if a Christian didn't want that—"but rather that ye may prophesy." To prophesy is to give out the Word of God, to speak it simply and to speak it intelligently.

He makes a distinction between the gifts which the Spirit gives and the fruit of the Spirit. The fruit of the Spirit is love, joy, peace, etc., which are more important than the gifts of the Spirit. Some very sincere people say to me, "Dr. McGee, I am going to pray that you receive the gift of the Spirit." I tell them I appreciate their interest, but I would rather they would pray that I may have the fruit of the Spirit. I wish I could see more fruit of the Spirit in the lives of the believers and in myself. I would like to see more love. That is the essential thing, and that is the fruit of the Holy Spirit. Only the Spirit of God can produce fruit in our lives.

"But rather that ye may prophesy." Actually, Paul was trying to get the Corinthians off this preoccupation with tongues. In effect he is saying to them in this whole section, "Cool it, brethren, don't go off into fanaticism or an emotional binge. Hold all things in their right proportion." In the previous chapter he said that tongues will cease. They will stop. That is the same word that we see posted on the highway. A traffic officer once told me that s-t-o-p means stop! I am afraid a great many folk do not understand what Paul is saying here: "Whether there be tongues, they shall stop." It was Dr. A. T. Robertson who made this statement: "Tongues seem to have ceased first of all the gifts." Chrysostom, one of the early church fathers, writing in the third or fourth century, stated: "This whole passage is very obscure; but the obscurity arises from our ignorance of the facts described, which, though familiar to those to whom the apostle wrote, have ceased to occur."

It is interesting to note that Jesus never spoke in tongues. There is no record of the apostles speaking in tongues after Pentecost. We do not have a historical record of Paul speaking in tongues or any sermon delivered in a tongue—although we know from verse 18 that Paul did speak in tongues because he said, "I thank my God, I speak with tongues more than ye all." I did not realize the import of this statement until I was in Turkey. I visited the ruins of seven churches there, and obviously Paul had preached in all of them; then going way out into the interior, into Anatolia, I realized that Paul had walked across that section—all the way from Tarsus, his hometown. It is a distance of hundreds of miles, and in that section there was tribe after tribe speaking different languages. I have often wondered how Paul was able to speak to them. Well, he spoke as the apostles did on the Day of Pentecost. Every man heard him speak in his own tongue. He probably said to the Corinthians, "If you want tongues, go out on the mission field and start speaking in the languages of those people."

Today God has raised up certain organizations like the Wycliffe Bible Translators who are attempting to translate the Bible into all the known tongues of the world. That, my friend, is the greatest tongues movement that I know anything about!

We know that at one time Paul was caught up to the third heaven. He tells us that he heard *unspeakable* words. I don't think those were *unknown* words or unknown tongues; they were words that he was not permitted to speak. Tongues are not a rapturous, ecstatic, mysterious language. They are not a mixed-up medley of rhapsody. Tongues were foreign languages. On the Day of Pentecost the apostles spoke in foreign languages so that every man there heard the gospel in his own language.

Now notice that chapter 14 is an extension of the love chapter. It begins: "Follow after charity [love], and desire spiritual gifts, but rather that ye may prophesy."

For he that speaketh in an unknown tongue speaketh not unto men, but unto God: for no man understandeth him; howbeit in the spirit he speaketh mysteries [1 Cor. 14:2].

Note that the word *unknown* is in italics in your Bible, and that means it is not in the original Greek. Nowhere in the Bible does it speak of unknown tongues. It should read: "For he that speaketh in a tongue speaketh not unto men, but unto God: for no man understandeth him; howbeit in the spirit he speaketh mysteries." Because nobody will understand him, he is not to speak in a language that is unknown to the group—unless somebody there can interpret.

We will see in this chapter that there are three gifts which Paul emphasizes: prophecy, tongues, and the interpretation of tongues. Have you ever noticed that there is very little reference to tongues in the Bible except in these three chapters? There are references to it in Mark 16:17 and Acts 2:3–4, 11; 10:46; 19:6. Cornelius and his household spoke in tongues. The disciples of John in Ephesus spoke in tongues after Paul had preached the gospel to them. We find, therefore, that tongues were used at the institution of the dispensation of grace. Every time tongues were used, they were used in that connection. There was speaking in tongues on the Day of Pentecost when the gospel went to the nation of Israel. There was speaking in tongues at the home of Cornelius when the gospel was opened to the Gentiles. There was speaking in tongues in Ephesus when the gospel moved out into the uttermost parts of the earth. Those are the three instances.

"For he that speaketh in a tongue speaketh not unto men, but unto God: for no man understandeth him; howbeit in the spirit he speaketh mysteries." That is, he doesn't understand it.

> **But he that prophesieth speaketh unto men to edification, and exhortation, and comfort [1 Cor. 14:3].**

Paul is emphasizing the gift of prophecy. He asks them not to go into the tongues which were delighting them, but to speak the Word of God which is for edification, for comfort, and for exhortation.

> **He that speaketh in an unknown tongue edifieth himself; but he that prophesieth edifieth the church [1 Cor. 14:4].**

The tongue, when it is exercised by the individual, is a selfish sort of gift, but prophesying, or teaching, is for the edification of the church.

> **I would that ye all spake with tongues, but rather that ye prophesied: for greater is he that prophesieth than he that speaketh with tongues, except he interpret, that the church may receive edifying [1 Cor. 14:5].**

To prophesy is to give forth the Word of God. The important thing is not a tongues meeting but a Bible study. "He that prophesieth" is one that teaches. No one is to speak in tongues unless there is someone there to interpret so learning can take place.

Now, brethren, if I come unto you speaking with tongues, what shall I profit you, except I shall speak to you either by revelation, or by knowledge, or by prophesying, or by doctrine? [1 Cor. 14:6].

Paul is saying, "If I don't make any sense when I come to talk to you, what is the use of my coming?"

And even things without life giving sound, whether pipe or harp, except they give a distinction in the sounds, how shall it be known what is piped or harped?

For if the trumpet give an uncertain sound, who shall prepare himself to the battle? [1 Cor. 14:7–8].

I have often thought that I could be a musician if I could do with a musical instrument what the "unknown tongues" folk do with sounds. Although I cannot read music and have no ear for it, I could just toot away on a horn. But of course it would just be a meaningless noise. Even a lifeless instrument like that is to have meaning in this world.

"If the trumpet give an uncertain sound, who shall prepare himself to the battle?" The trumpet was used to alert the troops for battle. And, my friend, today we need a clear-cut presentation of the gospel.

So likewise ye, except ye utter by the tongue words easy to be understood, how shall it be known what is spoken? for ye shall speak into the air [1 Cor. 14:9].

Paul says in effect, "Let's get off this kick. Let's start making sense, if you don't mind."

There are, it may be, so many kinds of voices in the world, and none of them is without signification.

Therefore if I know not the meaning of the voice, I shall be unto him that speaketh a barbarian, and he that

speaketh shall be a barbarian unto me. Even so ye,
forasmuch as ye are zealous of spiritual gifts, seek that
ye may excel to the edifying of the church [1 Cor.
14:10–12].

There are many languages in the world. However, there cannot be
communication between people who do not speak the same language.
If you speak in a language that no one in the church can understand,
how can this edify the people in the church? That is the important
issue. Does it edify the church? Does it build up the believers?

Wherefore let him that speaketh in an unknown tongue
pray that he may interpret [1 Cor. 14:13].

Anything that is said in a tongue should be interpreted. Otherwise it
does not make any sense to anyone. If the speaker cannot interpret,
then there must be someone else there who has the gift of interpretation.

For if I pray in an unknown tongue, my spirit prayeth,
but my understanding is unfruitful [1 Cor. 14:14].

That, my friend, is the answer to those who say that they speak in
tongues for their private devotions. If the "understanding is unfruitful," you don't get a spiritual lift out of it; that is, the Holy Spirit is not
ministering to you. If you get a lift, it is merely psychological. Paul
says your understanding is unfruitful.

What is it then? I will pray with the spirit, and I will
pray with the understanding also: I will sing with the
spirit, and I will sing with the understanding also.

Else when thou shalt bless with the spirit, how shall he
that occupieth the room of the unlearned say Amen at
thy giving of thanks, seeing he understandeth not what
thou sayest? [1 Cor. 14:15–16].

In other words, say something profitable so a brother can say "amen" to it.

For thou verily givest thanks well, but the other is not edified.

I thank my God, I speak with tongues more than ye all:

Yet in the church I had rather speak five words with my understanding, that by my voice I might teach others also, than ten thousand words in an unknown tongue [1 Cor. 14:17–19].

Now I think Paul means that, as a missionary, he had spoken in at least a dozen different tongues—and probably that could be multiplied by four or five. When he was out on the mission field with a foreign tribe, they couldn't understand his language and he couldn't understand theirs. Then he spoke to them in their tongue. He made sense to them, but it didn't make sense to Paul himself. But when he is in the church where there are believers who speak the same language as he does, he will speak in a tongue that everyone can understand.

Brethren, be not children in understanding: howbeit in malice be ye children, but in understanding be men [1 Cor. 14:20].

He is chiding the Corinthians again. He has called them carnal— babes in Christ. Now he tells them not to act like children.

In the law it is written, With men of other tongues and other lips will I speak unto this people; and yet for all that will they not hear me, saith the Lord [1 Cor. 14:21].

You see he *does* mean a language that is understood. He says, "I am going to speak to another people in *their* tongue."

> Wherefore tongues are for a sign, not to them that believe, but to them that believe not: but prophesying serveth not for them that believe not, but for them which believe [1 Cor. 14:22].

This is what he is saying: "When I went out to the mission field [let's say Antioch in Pisidia], they were speaking a different language, so I spoke to them in their own tongue. And when I presented the gospel to them in their own language, they believed. Now when I meet with these folk in the land of Israel, I speak in the language they know and I know. Therefore I am prophesying. That is, I am teaching the Word of God to them."

ORDER IN LOCAL CHURCH FOR EXERCISE OF ANY GIFT

> If therefore the whole church be come together into one place, and all speak with tongues, and there come in those that are unlearned, or unbelievers, will they not say that ye are mad? [1 Cor. 14:23].

We do not want a stranger to step into the church and think he has entered into a group of people who have gone mad. If there is one thing we need today, it is the logical, meaningful presentation of the Word of God. People in this world are intelligent; they are scientific; they are sophisticated. They want a logical message which can be understood. The Word of God needs to be presented so it can be understood.

> But if all prophesy, and there come in one that believeth not, or one unlearned, he is convinced of all, he is judged of all:
>
> And thus are the secrets of his heart made manifest; and so falling down on his face, he will worship God, and report that God is in you of a truth [1 Cor. 14:24–25].

In other words, if you are preaching the Word of God and an unbeliever comes in, he will come under conviction and be converted.

> **How is it then, brethren? when ye come together, every one of you hath a psalm, hath a doctrine, hath a tongue, hath a revelation, hath an interpretation. Let all things be done unto edifying [1 Cor. 14:26].**

If there is going to be any speaking in a tongue, there must be an interpreter there, and the message must be edifying. A former student of mine, who had been a Roman Catholic, went into a tongues meeting and recited part of a mass in Latin. When he sat down, another man rose to interpret. He went on to say this, that, and the other thing. Then this friend of mine got up and said, "I just want you to know that *that* is not what I said. I gave you the Latin mass." And as he started to tell them what he had really said, the ushers hustled him out of the meeting and told him not to come back. I don't blame them for that, and I do not think it was proper for my friend to do that. I simply tell this to emphasize the fact that speaking in a tongue may be the least edifying and may even be a hoax.

> **If any man speak in an unknown tongue, let it be by two, or at the most by three, and that by course; and let one interpret.**
>
> **But if there be no interpreter, let him keep silence in the church; and let him speak to himself, and to God [1 Cor. 14:27–28].**

Not only must there be edification, but there must be order. If someone is going to speak in a tongue, there must be an interpreter, and the message must make sense in conformity with the Word of God. If it is otherwise, the Spirit of God is not in it—you may be sure of that. If no interpreter is there, or if two or three have already spoken, the one wanting to speak in a tongue is to be silent. He can go off somewhere and speak by himself.

Let the prophets speak two or three, and let the other judge.

If any thing be revealed to another that sitteth by, let the first hold his peace [1 Cor. 14:29–30].

There were prophets in the church of that day, and they could speak prophetically. We know that the daughters of Philip prophesied (see Acts 21:9). In the same chapter we are told that Agabus also prophesied. We don't have that gift of foretelling the future anymore. Even the weatherman doesn't do very well in the area of prediction!

For ye may all prophesy one by one, that all may learn, and all may be comforted [1 Cor. 14:31].

They may all prophesy one by one. Everyone can have something to say about the Word of God. I have been greatly blessed by statements that some folk have made in testimony meetings.

And the spirits of the prophets are subject to the prophets.

For God is not the author of confusion, but of peace, as in all churches of the saints [1 Cor. 14:32–33].

A church service is to be orderly.

Let your women keep silence in the churches: for it is not permitted unto them to speak; but they are commanded to be under obedience, as also saith the law [1 Cor. 14:34].

Now what is he talking about here? Tongues. He is not saying that a woman is not to speak in church; he is saying that she is not to speak in tongues in the church. My friend, if you take the women out of the tongues movement, it would die overnight. You may say, "That's not a nice thing to say." I know it's not nice, but it is true.

> And if they will learn any thing, let them ask their husbands at home: for it is a shame for women to speak in the church.

> What? came the word of God out from you? or came it unto you only? [1 Cor. 14:35–36].

The Word of God came *to* them, of course.

> If any man think himself to be a prophet, or spiritual, let him acknowledge that the things that I write unto you are the commandments of the Lord.

> But if any man be ignorant, let him be ignorant [1 Cor. 14:37–38].

This is the real test. If a man today says that he is a prophet or that he is spiritual—because he can speak in tongues—let him acknowledge that what Paul is saying here is a commandment of the Lord.

> Wherefore, brethren, covet to prophesy, and forbid not to speak with tongues.

> Let all things be done decently and in order [1 Cor. 14:39–40].

Here again we are encouraged to covet the best gift. Evidently teaching the Word of God is the best one, and I thank God for that.

"Let all things be done decently and in order." This is a great principle. When I attended a tongues meeting in the South, I must confess that I could see neither rhyme nor reason in the entire service. It was all in confusion—not even an organized confusion, but *hopeless* confusion. Paul says that this is not the way things of God should be carried on.

This brings us to the conclusion of this section. If you have disagreed with me, I trust you will not fall out with me, but that you will search this Scripture. If I am wrong, pray for me.

CHAPTER 15

THEME: Resurrection

We have come to a chapter that can be classified as one of the most important and crucial chapters of the Bible. If you would select ten of the greatest chapters of the Bible—which men have done from the beginning of the Christian era—you will find that 1 Corinthians 15 will be on your list and has been on practically all the lists ever made. It is that important. It is so important that it actually answers the first heresy of the church, which was the denial of the bodily resurrection of the Lord Jesus Christ.

In this chapter Paul is coming to the third great spirituality. You will recall that first he dealt with carnalities. He dealt with those things which seemed so important to the Corinthians and still seem so important to us today. Then Paul turned from the carnalities to the spiritualities. How wonderful it is to know that every believer has a *gift* from the Holy Spirit. I can't think of anything more thrilling than to know that God has given you and me a gift to function in this world and that we are to be partners with Jesus Christ in the tremendous enterprise of making Him known!

Then Paul goes on to the great love chapter. All gifts are to be exercised in love, and love is a fruit of the Holy Spirit. It isn't something that we can work up. It is given to us. Above everything else we need to see love, this fruit of the Spirit, in the life of a believer.

Now we come to the third great spirituality, which is the fact of the resurrection of Jesus Christ and our own resurrection. The glory of the Christian faith is that it never views life as ending with death. This life is not all there is. The Christian faith always looks beyond the sunset to the sunrise. It looks out yonder into eternity—and what a hop it offers! This is another factor which gives meaning and purpose to life. I expect to live an eternity. I am not in a hurry to get there, and I want to stay in this life as long as I can because I think that this is the place of service. I think this is the place of preparation. I think that rewards are determined by what we do down here, and I want to get a few good works on my side of the ledger. That is why I would like to stay here and serve Him as long as He will allow me to stay. We used to sing a song, "Will there be any stars in my crown?" I don't hear that sung anymore. Why not? Well, it is because people are trying to be the star down here. Oh, my friend, that we might get the tremendous view which the resurrection of Jesus Christ should give to the believer. We have lost sight of the Ascension, and we have our minds on the incidentals. This adds up to one tragedy after another in the lives of professing Christians.

This great resurrection chapter actually deals with the gospel. It shows that the most important part of the gospel is the resurrection of Christ. Frankly, without that, everything else—even the death of Christ—is meaningless. He was delivered for our offenses and was raised again for our justification according to Romans 4:25. In His death He subtracted our sins, but in His resurrection He gave to us a sure, abundant entrance into heaven. We stand in His righteousness. He was delivered for our offenses, but He was raised again for our justification (our righteousness).

Before we get into this chapter, it would be well to define and delineate very sharply the meaning of the Resurrection. The Resurrection is not spiritual, but it is physical. The word is *anastasis nekrōn*, which means the "standing up of a corpse." These bodies of ours are to be raised; the Resurrection in Scripture always refers to the body. *Anastasis* means "to stand up." *Histemi* means "to cause to stand." *Ana* means the standing up of the body. It cannot refer to a spiritual resurrection.

C. S. Lewis, the brilliant Oxford don, ridiculed the liberals in England in his day. They would talk about the Resurrection being spiritual, so Lewis would ask, "What position does a spirit take when it stands up?" That is a question for the liberal to kick around for a while. Scripture teaches that the Resurrection means to stand up.

In Paul's day, in Corinth and in the Roman world, there were three philosophies concerning death and life after death. There was Stoicism, which taught that the soul merged into deity at death. There was, therefore, a destruction of the personality. Such a concept makes the Resurrection a nonentity. Then there was the Epicurean philosophy, which was materialistic. It taught that there was no existence beyond death. Death was the end of existence. The third was Platonism which taught the immortality of the soul, believing in a process like a transmigration. You still find that teaching in Platonism today in the religions of India and in the cults of America. It denies the bodily resurrection. Because of these philosophies, when Paul mentioned the Resurrection while he was in Athens, they thought he was talking about a new God.

We need to understand very clearly that Paul is not talking about a *spiritual* resurrection. The soul does not die. The minute a body dies, the person goes somewhere. If the person is a child of God, to be absent from the body means to be present with the Lord (see 2 Cor. 5:6–8). If a person is not a child of God, then he goes to the place of torment—our Lord labeled it that.

The divisions of this chapter are as follows:

1. The prominence of the Resurrection in the gospel—verses 1–4
2. The proofs of the Resurrection—verses 5–19
3. The parade of the Resurrection—verses 20–28
4. The program and pattern of the Resurrection—verses 29–50
5. The power of the Resurrection—verses 51–58

PROMINENCE OF RESURRECTION IN THE GOSPEL

Paul states that the Resurrection is part of the gospel; in fact, there is no gospel without the Resurrection. Dr. Machen says that Christianity does not rest on a set of ideas or creeds, but on facts. The gospel is not the Ten Commandments or the Sermon on the Mount. The gospel is a series of facts concerning a person and that person is Jesus Christ.

Now listen to the way Paul states it:

> **Moreover, brethren, I declare unto you the gospel which I preached unto you, which also ye have received, and wherein ye stand;**
>
> **By which also ye are saved, if ye keep in memory what I preached unto you, unless ye have believed in vain.**

> For I delivered unto you first of all that which I also received, how that Christ died for our sins according to the scriptures;
>
> And that he was buried, and that he rose again the third day according to the scriptures [1 Cor. 15:1–4].

The question sometimes arises whether the gospel originated with Paul. He says, "I delivered unto you . . . that which I received." From whom did he receive it and where? He received it out yonder in that Arabian desert where the Lord took him and taught him. When Paul was confronted by the Lord on the Damascus road, he did not know that Jesus was back from the dead. He asked, ". . . Who art thou, Lord? . . . (Acts 9:5). He didn't dream that "the Lord" was Jesus. Paul himself had to be convinced of the resurrection of Jesus Christ. He didn't think it up. He received it.

Paul says that he declares the gospel to them. What is the gospel? "Christ died for our sins according to the scriptures; And that he was buried, and that he rose again the third day according to the scriptures." That is the gospel. These are the facts. My friend, there is no gospel apart from those three facts. That is what the gospel is. Jesus Christ died for you and for me. He was buried and He rose again. That is gospel—it's good news.

Now suppose that you come to me today and say, "Teacher, I have good news for you—I would like to see you become a millionaire." I would say, "Well, that would be nice." Then you would tell me your plan. You would say, "You get a job, and in a thousand years you will be worth a million dollars." I would say, "Well, I sure would like to have a million dollars; I could use it to get the gospel out, but if you think by my working I can make a million dollars, you are wrong. That's not good news. In fact, it is bad news!" However, suppose you come to me and say, "I have discovered someone who was interested in you. In fact, he loved you so much that when he died he left you a million dollars!" That, my friend, would be good news!

The gospel does not tell us something that we must do. The gospel tells us what Jesus Christ has already done for us. He died for our sins according to the Scriptures, He was buried, He rose again the third day.

He died. That is a historical fact. Very few would deny that. He was buried—that needs to be added. Why is that so important? It proves that He didn't just disappear. It means that they actually, literally had His body. Nicodemus and Joseph of Arimathaea and the others who saw Him crucified knew who He was. They knew it was Jesus. They buried Jesus. That is very important. It confirms His death.

He rose again the third day according to the Scriptures. The Resurrection is a part of the gospel. The tomb was empty. That is the proof. The gospel is that Jesus died, was buried, and rose again. This is the first proof.

There is another proof of the Resurrection, and that is the experience of the Corinthians. Let's listen to it again. "Moreover, brethren, I declare unto you the gospel which I preached unto you, which also ye have received, and wherein ye stand; By which also ye are saved, if ye keep in memory what I preached unto you, unless ye have believed in vain" (vv. 1–2). "Unless ye have believed in vain"—that is, unless it was an empty faith.

There is a faith that is an empty faith, of course. But he says, "By which also ye are *saved*." The church is the proof of the Resurrection.

There were eleven discouraged men in Jerusalem or its environs. They were ready to go back to fishing. They had just gone through enough trouble. If Jesus was dead, they didn't want the body out of the grave. They wanted it to stay there. They wouldn't go break a Roman seal and face a Roman guard to steal a body which could only bring them more trouble. Then what happened? Word came to them that Jesus Christ had risen from the dead! That fact transformed these men. That revolutionary fact brought the church into existence. Through nineteen centuries there have been millions of people who have said that Jesus Christ is alive. You simply cannot explain the church apart from the Resurrection. I am saved by the death and resurrection of Jesus. Without His resurrection I would have no gospel, no living Christ, no Savior. The existence of the body of believers is the second great proof of the Resurrection.

There is another proof. Notice that it says He died for our sins "according to the scriptures" and that He was buried and rose again the third day "according to the scriptures." What Scriptures? The Old Testament Scriptures. I would love to have been with Paul the apostle when he arrived in Europe and went to Philippi, Thessalonica, then down to Athens, and over to Corinth. I think he had with him a parchment which was the Old Testament. I imagine that when he went into a synagogue and mentioned the death of the Lord Jesus, the Jews said, "But this is not in our Scriptures." Then he would turn to the Book of Genesis and say, "I'd like to remind you about the offering of Isaac and how Abraham received him back from the 'dead'—he was ready to kill the boy. Now God spared not His own Son, but delivered Him up freely for us all." Then he would turn to the Mosaic system of sacrifice, to the five offerings in Leviticus, and show them how they pictured Christ, then to the great Day of Atonement and the two goats which pictured Christ's death and resurrection. Also he would cite Aaron's rod that budded and the Book of Jonah, which typifies resurrection. Then he would turn to Psalm 22 and Psalm 16. He would show them Isaiah 25 and in Isaiah 53 he would point out that He was wounded for our transgressions and He was bruised for our iniquities. All we like sheep have gone astray, we have turned everyone to his own way, and the Lord hath laid on Him the iniquity of all of us. So he could show them from the Old Testament Scriptures that Jesus Christ was to die and to rise again. The expectation of the Old Testament was not for this life only but also for the life that is to come.

There are some folk who say they do not believe in a "hereafter religion"; they want a here-and-now religion. May I say to you that I have both—a here-and-now religion and a hereafter religion.

PROOFS OF RESURRECTION—WITNESSES

Now as another proof of the Resurrection Paul lists a number of witnesses. You just can't get around witnesses. Any lawyer today would love to have as many witnesses for his position as Paul lists here as proofs of the Resurrection.

And that he was seen of Cephas, then of the twelve [1 Cor. 15:5].

He mentions Cephas first. This is, of course, Simon Peter, to whom Jesus appeared privately. You may ask, "What took place?" It is none of my business, and I guess it is none of yours. It is not recorded for us. Jesus appeared to Peter. After all, he had denied Him. Peter had to get things straightened out with the Lord. You see, our Lord is still in the footwashing business.

Then He was seen "of the twelve." Who are the Twelve? He appeared to Cephas privately, then He appeared to the ten (Judas was dead at this time). "The Twelve" was used as a collective term for the body of disciples. It does not necessarily imply that twelve disciples were present. However, when you put them all together and Paul joins them, you have twelve men.

After that, he was seen of above five hundred brethren at once; of whom the greater part remain unto this present, but some are fallen asleep [1 Cor. 15:6].

Jesus was seen of five hundred people at one time. I think this was up yonder around the Sea of Galilee. Remember that He had told them He would meet with them in Galilee. So I believe that His true followers went up to Galilee to meet Him there. As they traveled northward, I'm sure folk would ask them, "Now that Jesus is dead, are you going back to fishing?" They would answer, "No, Jesus is back from the dead and we're going up there to meet Him." There were five hundred of His followers who met Him there.

After that, he was seen of James; then of all the apostles.

And last of all he was seen of me also, as of one born out of due time [1 Cor. 15:7–8].

"He was seen of James"—this was probably a private interview. He was seen again by all the apostles. Lastly, He was seen by Paul. My friend, it is very difficult to argue with a man who has seen Him.

For I am the least of the apostles, that am not meet to be called an apostle, because I persecuted the church of God.

But by the grace of God I am what I am: and his grace which was bestowed upon me was not in vain; but I laboured more abundantly than they all: yet not I, but the grace of God which was with me [1 Cor. 15:9–10].

Paul calls himself the least of the apostles. He is being very modest here. Inspiration guarantees that this is a statement which came from his heart. My heart says, "Paul, you're great. I can't consider you the least of the apostles." But Paul says he isn't worthy to be called an apostle because he persecuted the church of God. He considered himself to be the chief of sinners. Yet he was the hardest worker of any of the apostles. But, very candidly, he tells us that it was the grace of God that enabled him to accomplish what he did.

Therefore whether it were I or they, so we preach, and so ye believed [1 Cor. 15:11].

I am tired of men talking about being Christians and denying the facts of the gospel. You are not a Christian if you deny the death, burial, and resurrection of Christ. You have a perfect right to deny these things if you wish, but you have no right then to call yourself a Christian. It says here that when these Corinthians heard the gospel, they believed, and that is when they became Christians.

This is so crucial and so critical that we are going to review it to emphasize it. What is the gospel? It is the good news that Christ died, was buried, and rose again on the third day. He didn't vanish or disappear. He rose again. The tomb is empty. Jesus Christ is alive today. These are the historical facts. The gospel is not a theory, not an idea, not a religion. The gospel consists of objective facts. This is the gospel which Paul preached. It is not simply a subjective experience which Paul had; it is fact.

It tells us in verse 1 that the Corinthians received it and in verse 11 that they believed it. What does it mean to receive Christ? John

1:11–13 tells us, "He came unto his own, and his own received him not. But as many as received him, to them gave he power to become the sons of God, even to them that believe on his name: Which were born, not of blood, nor of the will of the flesh, nor of the will of man, but of God." To receive Christ means to believe on His name. Our first verse says of the gospel relative to the Corinthians, "which also ye have received, and wherein ye stand." That was their current state. They stood in a living faith in relationship with a living Lord Jesus Christ. Where do you stand today?

The second verse says, "By which also ye are saved." The gospel does not save if it is just a head knowledge. It is not just a nodding assent to the facts. It is the One of whom the gospel speaks who does the saving—Christ saves. When you accept the facts of the gospel, when you put your faith in Christ absolutely, then you are saved. As Spurgeon put it, "It is not thy joy in Christ that saves thee. It is not thy hope in Christ that saves thee. it is Christ. It is not even thy faith in Christ, though that be the instrument." It is Christ's blood and merit that saves.

The gospel was preached to the Corinthians. Paul said, "You received it, you stand in it, and you are saved." Then he adds, "Unless ye have believed in vain." If their faith does not rest upon the facts, then it is a vain faith, of no effect, and theirs is not a genuine conversion. Faith itself has no merit. The important thing is the object of your faith—in whom you believe. Have you trusted a Savior who died, who was buried, and who rose again from the dead?

We spoke of the significance of the testimony of the Old Testament Scriptures as an evidence of the Resurrection. Then there were the witnesses who were alive at the time Paul was writing: Cephas, the twelve, the five hundred, James, all the apostles, and finally he himself, all of whom saw the resurrected Christ. Of himself he says, "as of one born out of due time." That is, his was not a late birth but an abortion, a premature birth. He is a picture of that remnant which is to be saved after the church is removed from this earth.

Now if Christ be preached that he rose from the dead,

how say some among you that there is no resurrection of the dead? [1 Cor. 15:12].

Some of these people with backgrounds of Stoicism, Epicureanism, and Platonism were denying the Resurrection. It wasn't that they were specifically denying the resurrection of Jesus Christ, but they did not believe in any resurrection at all.

Now Paul begins a series of "ifs"—"if Christ be not risen." Paul faced the fact. My Christian friend, don't hide your head like an ostrich under the sand and say, "Well, we can't be sure about the Resurrection, so let's not say too much about it. Let's walk as if we were walking on eggshells." My friend, I am on a foundation; that foundation is the Rock, and the Rock is Christ. He came back from the dead. Paul is not afraid that Christ might not have risen from the dead. He puts down these "ifs" as a demonstration of the importance of the resurrection of Jesus Christ.

But if there be no resurrection of the dead, then is Christ not risen [1 Cor. 15:13].

If there is no resurrection from the dead, then Christ is not risen. They are linked together. And it is on the basis of the resurrection of Christ—Paul is going to say later on—that Jesus Christ is the firstfruits. That means there will be more to follow. He is the firstfruits, and later at His coming there will be the resurrection of those who are His.

And if Christ be not risen, then is our preaching vain, and your faith is also vain [1 Cor. 15:14].

Perhaps you belong to a church which denies that Christ arose from the dead. If Christ is not bodily risen from the dead, then our preaching is vain. Not only that, but our faith is vain also. You might just as well drop your church membership. It's no good. There is no reason to go to church or to hear a sermon if Christ is not raised from the dead.

Yea, and we are found false witnesses of God; because we have testified of God that he raised up Christ: whom he raised not up, if so be that the dead rise not [1 Cor. 15:15].

All the apostles were liars if Christ had not risen. Every one of these men was a false witness if Christ is still in the grave. Have you ever noticed that men do not die for that which they know to be a lie? Men *do* die for a lie, but they think it is the truth. For instance, millions of men died for Hitler because they believed in him. The apostles testified that they saw the risen Christ, and they were willing to die for that declaration. I'll let you decide if they were right or wrong. But men do *not* die for what they *know* is a lie.

For if the dead rise not, then is not Christ raised:

And if Christ be not raised, your faith is vain; ye are yet in your sins [1 Cor. 15:16–17].

If Christ is not raised, then, my friend, you are a lost, hell-doomed sinner, and that is all you can ever be. If Christ be not raised, every one of us is still in our sins.

Then they also which are fallen asleep in Christ are perished [1 Cor. 15:18].

There have been millions upon millions of believers who have died trusting Christ as their Savior. If Christ is not risen, then every one of them has perished.

If in this life only we have hope in Christ, we are of all men most miserable [1 Cor. 15:19].

May I say to you that I think Christianity is a here-and-now religion. Paul makes that clear in the sixth chapter of Romans. But Christianity is also a hereafter religion. If Christ be not raised, we have been deluded and we are about the most miserable people in this world today. But we're not! We're rejoicing!

That is the end of Paul's *"ifs."* Will you face up to the possibilities which he presents? Go through the *"ifs"* logically and you will see that the human family is lost and hopeless if Christ had not been raised from the dead.

PARADE OF THE RESURRECTION

So I want to join Paul as he declares the Resurrection—

But now is Christ risen from the dead, and become the firstfruits of them that slept [1 Cor. 15:20].

Christ is the firstfruits. In the Old Testament they had the festival of firstfruits when they would bring the first sheaf of grain to the Lord. This meant that there would be more to come, otherwise it couldn't be the firstfruits. The fulfillment of that is in the resurrection of Jesus Christ. He came back from the dead in a glorified body. And He is the only one who has come back from the dead in a glorified body.

For since by man came death, by man came also the resurrection of the dead.

For as in Adam all die, even so in Christ shall all be made alive [1 Cor. 15:21–22].

After the festival of the firstfruits came Pentecost, which was fifty days later. That found its fulfillment in Pentecost in the New Testament when the church began. But it will find its ultimate fulfillment when Christ comes for His own and they shall all rise to meet Him in the air. That will be the real Pentecost. A Pentecostal brother of mine said, "You know, Brother McGee, I'm expecting a Pentecost." I shocked him when I said, "I'm looking for Pentecost too." He said, "Oh, you don't mean it!" I said, "I don't mean it like you mean it— you think you are going to repeat the Day of Pentecost down here. The

Pentecost I am waiting for is when the Lord Jesus comes to take His church out of His world." Christ is the firstfruits.

But every man in his own order: Christ the firstfruits; afterward they that are Christ's at his coming [1 Cor. 15:23].

How wonderful that is! "Christ is risen from the dead, and become the firstfruits of them that slept"—meaning the sleep of death. "For since by man came death [that man is Adam], by man came also the resurrection of the dead." "In Adam all die"—the proof that you are in the family of Adam is that you are going to die unless the Lord comes to take you in the Rapture. "Even so in Christ shall all be made alive." Jesus is the Resurrection and the Life.

"But every man in his own order." There is not a general resurrection day. It is interesting that the Reformers recovered a great deal of the truth of the Bible, but they didn't recover all of it. We are living in a day when there is much Bible study in the field of eschatology; that is, the doctrine of the last things—prophecy. It is a study of prophecy. In times when great truths are being recovered one also finds a lot of heresy and just plain "nutty" ideas. There is a lot of false teaching about prophecy, largely because of ignorance of the whole scope of Scripture. I firmly believe that the Book of Revelation should not be taught unless one has studied the other books of the Bible first. Prophecy is important, but it is not everything. The great Reformers recovered much Bible truth, but they missed this teaching of the Bible that every man will be raised in his own order, that there is not a general resurrection day.

Christ is the firstfruits, and then "afterward they that are Christ's at his coming." What is He coming for? He is coming for His church, my friend.

Then cometh the end, when he shall have delivered up the kingdom to God, even the Father; when he shall have put down all rule and all authority and power [1 Cor. 15:24].

"Then cometh the end"—the end of what? The end of the age. How will the age end? There will come the Great Tribulation, and then there is going to be the millennial Kingdom here on the earth. Satan will be released again for a little while, then he will be cast forever into the lake of fire, and the Lord Jesus Christ will establish His Kingdom forever. That will be the eternal Kingdom. Actually, the eternal Kingdom is a further projection of the millennial Kingdom, only the millennial Kingdom will be a time of trial. "Then cometh the end, when he shall have delivered up the kingdom to God." When will this take place? At the end of the millennial Kingdom, Christ will put down all rule and all authority and power.

> **For he must reign, till he hath put all enemies under his feet [1 Cor. 15:25].**

That is Satan.

> **The last enemy that shall be destroyed is death [1 Cor. 15:26].**

I'll be glad when we get rid of that fellow!

> **For he hath put all things under his feet. But when he saith all things are put under him, it is manifest that he is excepted, which did put all things under him [1 Cor. 15:27].**

So Christ is not subject to God—but wait a minute, notice what the next verse says.

> **And when all things shall be subdued unto him, then shall the Son also himself be subject unto him that put all things under him, that God may be all in all [1 Cor. 15:28].**

This means that when Christ has completed His millennial reign here upon this earth and has established His eternal reign (I believe that He will turn over to David His throne on the earth), then He will return back to His place in the Godhead where He was in the beginning, so that "God may be all in all."

PROGRAM AND PATTERN OF THE RESURRECTION

Else what shall they do which are baptized for the dead, if the dead rise not at all? why are they then baptized for the dead? [1 Cor. 15:29].

"What shall they do"—that is, what shall they accomplish? We have already learned that the word *baptize* means identification with someone or something. In this case Paul is speaking of identification as a dead person. He asks, "What shall they accomplish which are baptized for the dead, if the dead rise not at all?" Why are they then identified as the dead? This does not imply that the Corinthian believers were being baptized for their dead relatives or friends. It means that they were baptized or identified with Christ Jesus—who had died for them and He was now risen from the dead. They were dead to the world but were alive to Christ.

And why stand we in jeopardy every hour?

I protest by your rejoicing which I have in Christ Jesus our Lord, I die daily [1 Cor. 15:30-31].

Paul is saying that if Christ be not raised from the dead, then they are foolish to put their lives in danger. However, since Christ *is* raised from the dead, believers are identified with Him. As Paul said to the believers at Rome, "Know ye not, that so many of us as were baptized into Jesus Christ were baptized into his death? Therefore we are buried with him by baptism into death: that like as Christ was raised up from the dead by the glory of the Father, even so we also should walk in newness of life" (Rom. 6:3-4). We are joined to a resurrected, living Christ. "Now if Christ was not resurrected, then," Paul says, "I am foolish to make the sacrifices I have made down here—my life stands in jeopardy every hour. I am constantly in danger of death."

If after the manner of men I have fought with beasts at Ephesus, what advantageth it me, if the dead rise not? let us eat and drink; for to-morrow we die [1 Cor. 15:32].

Paul asks, "Why should I be put in a lions' cage for my faith in Christ if Christ did not rise from the dead? I am identified—I am baptized—into His death. I am identified as a dead man because I am joined to a living Christ." Being identified with Christ in His death and resurrection is a tremendous fact! Let's not reduce it to some little water baptismal service that would be meaningless.

If Christ is not risen and if the dead will not be resurrected, then we might as well adopt the the hedonistic philosophy of the Epicureans who say, "Let us eat and drink; for to-morrow we die."

Be not deceived: evil communications corrupt good manners.

Awake to righteousness, and sin not; for some have not the knowledge of God: I speak this to your shame [1 Cor. 15:33–34].

The Corinthian believers were being deceived by those who questioned the Resurrection. They were listening to those who had plenty to say but no knowledge of God. Paul is saying that if they get the wrong information, they will act wrong. He admonishes them to stop sinning—because there *will* be a resurrection.

But some man will say, How are the dead raised up? and with what body do they come? [1 Cor. 15:35].

Paul will answer two questions: the *how* and the *what*. Men fail to distinguish the difference between the resurrection of the body and the immortality of the soul. Plato and Cicero argued from the immortality of the soul. Paul is arguing for the resurrection of the body. The Sadducees denied any resurrection, any life after death. And Christ Himself had answered them: "But as touching the resurrection of the dead, have ye not read that which was spoken unto you by God, saying, I am the God of Abraham, and the God of Isaac, and the God of Jacob? God is not the God of the dead, but of the living" (Matt. 22:31–32).

Paul has answered those who denied the resurrection of the body by the resurrection of Christ whose body was raised up.

Now the question is, "How can a body that dies be raised up again and be the same?" Paul says that we learn from nature that the bodies are not identical—they are the same but not identical.

> **Thou fool, that which thou sowest is not quickened, except it die [1 Cor. 15:36].**

The answer to the first question: the *how*. He says in effect, "If you only had sense enough to see it, you would see that in a seed which is planted, there is dissolution and continuity—a seed that is planted will produce seeds which are essentially the same as that seed. But the seed itself has died and disintegrated, so that the seed it produces is not the very seed that died. It is like that seed, but it is not the same seed. In the seed that is planted there is a disintegration and yet there is a continuity. It is a mystery, but it is not an impossibility."

What is death? Death is a separation. It is not the ending of the spirit or of the personality. These do not die. The real "you" goes on to be with the Lord if you are a child of God. It is the body that disintegrates. Death is a separation of the body from the individual, from the person. The body disintegrates, decays, decomposes. Dust to dust and ashes to ashes applies only to the body.

Paul now answers the second question: *What* body is raised up?

> **And that which thou sowest, thou sowest not that body that shall be, but bare grain, it may chance of wheat, or of some other grain [1 Cor. 15:37].**

The sowing of grain is the illustration. Christ is the firstfruits, then we'll be coming along later. We are waiting for the rapture of the church when Christ takes the believers out of the world. If at the time of the Rapture we are already dead, we will be raised up. If we are still alive at the time of the Rapture, we'll be caught up and changed. The seed, you see, does not provide itself with a new body, neither does the sower, but God provides it:

> **But God giveth it a body as it hath pleased him, and to every seed his own body [1 Cor. 15:38].**

Then Paul moves into another area. All of this is the mystery of life. Actually the mystery of life is greater than the mystery of death. When you sow wheat, wheat comes up—not barley or corn. That little grain that forms on the stalk is like the one you sowed—not identical, but certainly very similar.

Now he moves from the area of botany to zoology.

> **All flesh is not the same flesh: but there is one kind of flesh of men, another flesh of beasts, another of fishes, and another of birds [1 Cor. 15:39].**

The difference between a dead body and the resurrection body is greater than the difference between men and beasts, fish and birds. Paul says that all flesh is not the same flesh.

> **There are also celestial bodies, and bodies terrestrial: but the glory of the celestial is one, and the glory of the terrestrial is another.**
>
> **There is one glory of the sun, and another glory of the moon, and another glory of the stars: for one star differeth from another star in glory [1 Cor. 15:40–41].**

Now he has moved into the realm of astronomy and says that all the bodies of the solar system are not the same. The sun is not the same material as the moon, neither is it the same as the stars. The stars differ from each other. There is a solar system, a stellar system, planets, and suns.

> **So also is the resurrection of the dead. It is sown in corruption; it is raised in incorruption [1 Cor. 15:42].**

You see, the body that was given Adam was always subject to death. Although he would not have died if he had not sinned, his body would have been subject to death. However, by resurrection we get a body that is incorruptible.

> **It is sown in dishonor; it is raised in glory; it is sown in weakness; it is raised in power [1 Cor. 15:43].**

We will get glory and color and beauty and power—all of these things—with the new body.

> **It is sown a natural body; it is raised a spiritual body. There is a natural body, and there is a spiritual body [1 Cor. 15:44].**

Many years ago in the city of New York (in fact, it was way back in the day when liberalism was called modernism, back in the 1920s) they had an argument about whether resurrection was spiritual. The liberal even today claims it's spiritual. He doesn't believe in bodily resurrection at all. A very famous Greek scholar from the University of Chicago read a paper on the passage from this verse. His paper put the emphasis on the word *spiritual*. He concluded by saying, "Now, brethren, you can see that resurrection is spiritual because it says it's spiritual." The liberals all applauded, and somebody made a motion that they print that manuscript and circulate it. Well, a very fine Greek scholar was there, and he stood up. And when he stood up, all the liberals were a little uneasy. He could ask very embarrassing questions. He said, "I'd like to ask the author of the paper a question." Very reluctantly, the good doctor stood up. "Now, doctor, which is stronger, a noun or an adjective? A very simple question, but I'd like for you to answer it." He could see the direction he was going and didn't want to answer it, but he had to. "Well," he said, "a noun is stronger, of course." "Now doctor, I'm amazed that you presented the paper that you did today. You put the emphasis upon an adjective, and the strong word is the noun. Now let's look at that again. 'It is sown a natural body; it is raised a spiritual *body*.'" He said, "The only thing that is carried over in resurrection is the body. It's one kind of body when it dies, a natural body. It's raised a body, but a spiritual body, dominated now by the spirit—but it's still a body." And, you know, they never did publish that paper. They decided it would be better not to publish it. May I say to you, just a simple little exercise in grammar answered this great professor's whole manuscript and his entire argument which he presented at that time.

And so it is written, The first man Adam was made a living soul; the last Adam was made a quickening spirit [1 Cor. 15:45].

You see, the first man, Adam, was psychical—*psuchen* and *zosan* in the Greek. That means he was physical and psychological. The last Adam (Christ) is spiritual—*pneuma* or pneumatical, if you want the English equivalent.

Howbeit that was not first which is spiritual, but that which is natural; and afterward that which is spiritual.

The first man is of the earth, earthy: the second man is the Lord from heaven [1 Cor. 15:46-47].

The first man is of the earth and is earthy—*choikos*, meaning "clay," rubbish if you please. There is so much talk of ecology today. Who messed up this earth anyway? Man. Because man is earthy. Everything that is the refuse of man is rubbish. He is that kind of creature. He fills the garbage cans. But the Second Man is the Lord from heaven.

As is the earthy, such are they also that are earthy: and as is the heavenly, such are they also that are heavenly.

And as we have borne the image of the earthy, we shall also bear the image of the heavenly.

Now this I say, brethren, that flesh and blood cannot inherit the kingdom of God; neither doth corruption inherit incorruption [1 Cor. 15:48-50].

We are all earthy. We are from Adam and that is our condition. But we are also in Christ. We are joined to Him, and therefore we have a hope, the hope of the resurrection in an eternal body which will forever be with Christ. Today we bear the image of the earthy, but we look forward to the day when we will bear the image of the heavenly.

Flesh and blood cannot inherit the Kingdom of God. Our old bodies are not going to heaven—I'm glad of that. I would like to trade mine in. God is not going to send these bodies into a repair shop. Corruption cannot inherit incorruption. This body must be put into the ground, like a seed. It will come up a new body, a new tabernacle for us to live in. It will not be identical to the old body, and yet it will be like the old body.

Out here on the west coast there are many atheists who have their ashes scattered out over the Pacific Ocean after they die. In other words, they challenge God to try to put all of those atoms together again. Our bodies are made up of a few chemicals. Most of the body's composition is water, hydrogen, and oxygen, with other atoms thrown in with it. Do you think that God cannot bring those atoms together? Or maybe He wants to use other atoms. After all, hydrogen atoms are all very much alike. It wouldn't make any difference to me if He used other atoms to make my new body. What nonsense to discount the Resurrection because of this! Yet one of the foremost arguments against the possibility of resurrection is that God would not be able to regather all those atoms! My friend, since He made the body to begin with, He certainly can make another like it. He is God, isn't He? God will get your body together again whether it comes out of the grave or its ashes are scattered out there in the ocean.

The first heresy in the church was the denial of the bodily resurrection. We see how Paul has shown the truth of the Resurrection. He has spoken against the three major philosophies of his day. Stoicism said the soul merged into Deity at death, and there was a destruction of personality. Paul says our bodies shall rise. Epicureanism said there was no existence beyond death. Paul says Jesus Christ was raised from the dead and our bodies, too, shall rise. Platonism believed in the immortality of the soul but denied the bodily resurrection. Paul says that our physical bodies shall be made alive as spiritual bodies.

POWER OF THE RESURRECTION

Behold, I shew you a mystery; We shall not all sleep, but we shall all be changed [1 Cor. 15:51].

What is a mystery? We have already discussed it several times. A mystery is something which had not been revealed in the Old Testament but is now revealed in the New Testament. It is something which you cannot learn by the eye-gate or the ear-gate. Nor has it entered into the heart of man—that is, it is not something many would have thought of. It is a fact which must be revealed by God.

"Behold, I shew you a mystery; We shall not all sleep"—we are not all going down through the doorway of death. "But we shall all be changed." Whether you die or don't die, you must still be changed, friend. Sometimes we hear people say, "I hope I am alive at the coming of Christ; so I will just go into His presence." Well, before any of us can go into His presence, we'll have to be changed.

In a moment, in the twinkling of an eye, at the last trump: for the trumpet shall sound, and the dead shall be raised incorruptible, and we shall be changed [1 Cor. 15:52].

"In a moment," in the smallest particle of time. The word is *en atomo* from which we get our word "atom." Scientists made a big mistake when they called that little fellow an atom. They thought they had found the smallest particle of matter, and now they can cut up the little atom like a railroad restaurant pie. It would have been better if we had named it a *stoicheion*, which means "a building block." Actually, Simon Peter uses this word in his second epistle when he says that the elements *(stoicheion)* shall melt with a fervent heat. And he wasn't even a scientist; he was a fisherman. But the Spirit of God knew a little about science!

We shall all be changed "in the twinkling of an eye." How long is that? Is a twinkle when the lid goes down or when it comes up, or is it both of them? Well, it simply means in a moment, in a fraction of a second. There won't even be time to say, "Here He comes" or "He is here!"

"At the last trump." What is that? That is His last call. The trumpet is His voice. John tells us in the Book of Revelation, "I was in the Spirit on the Lord's day, and heard behind me a great voice, as of a trumpet," and when he turned to see who was speaking, he saw Christ (see Rev. 1:10–13). So "at the last trump" is the voice of the Lord Jesus. On His last call to mankind, He will call the dead back to life. He said, ". . . Lazarus, come forth" (John 11:43). Someday He will say to me, "Vernon, come forth." And He will also call you by name.

"And the dead shall be raised incorruptible, and we shall be changed."

> **For this corruptible must put on incorruption, and this mortal must put on immortality [1 Cor. 15:53].**

Notice the word *must*—it is emphatic. We cannot go to heaven as we are now. We cannot go to heaven with the old bodies we have. We wouldn't be able to see what is really up there, nor could we hear the music. Our bodies are quite limited. We are almost deaf and blind as far as heaven is concerned. Even here on earth there is so little of the spectrum that we actually see and so little of the sounds that we actually hear. If we went to heaven in these old bodies, we would miss half of what was taking place. And, my friend, when I go up there, I don't want to miss a thing! Therefore I'm going to need a new body. "This corruptible must put on incorruption, and this mortal must put on immortality."

> **So when this corruptible shall have put on incorruption, and this mortal shall have put on immortality, then shall be brought to pass the saying that is written, Death is swallowed up in victory [1 Cor. 15:54].**

This is the victory of the Resurrection.

> **O death, where is thy sting? O grave, where is thy victory?**

The sting of death is sin; and the strength of sin is the law.

But thanks be to God, which giveth us the victory through our Lord Jesus Christ [1 Cor. 15:55–57].

I heard a Bible teacher say that since God has taken the sting out of death, it is like a bee that has his stinger removed. Well, I can't tell when a bee's stinger has been removed. I can't stop every bee and ask, "Say, do you have a stinger?" Therefore, I am afraid of every bee.

Death has lost its sting because we are to look way out beyond death. It is a doorway that opens up the vast regions of eternity. It starts us down the hallway, not of time, but of eternity. But I don't like going through that door.

"O grave, where is thy victory?" It looks as if the grave wins. Many a man has been a successful businessman, but death finally won over him. Many a politician gets elected to high office, even to the presidency, and then dies in office. They reach the heights, but death walks in on them and claims a victory. Death is an awful monster. However, Christ has been down through that way. Just as the ark went down into the Jordan River and over to the other side, so Christ has gone down through the waters of death for me, and He tells me, "I'm your Shepherd. Remember, I not only lead you through this life, but I'll lead you through the deep waters of death, and I will bring you into eternity." So like a little child I'm afraid, but I'll put my hand in His nail-pierced hand, and He will lead me to the other side. "O grave, where is thy victory?"

"The sting of death is sin." It is sin that has the real stinger.

"The strength of sin is the law." The law is the mirror that shows us we are sinners.

"But thanks be to God, which giveth us the victory." How? Because we are smart and clever and are overcomers? No, the victory is through our Lord Jesus Christ. Speaking of the tribulation saints, Revelation 12:11 says that they overcame Satan by the blood of the Lamb. That is the only way any of us will overcome.

Therefore, my beloved brethren, be ye stedfast, unmoveable, always abounding in the work of the Lord, forasmuch as ye know that your labour is not in vain in the Lord [1 Cor. 15:58].

I think this verse goes all the way back to chapter 1:9. "God is faithful [Oh, how faithful He is], by whom ye were called unto the fellowship of his Son Jesus Christ our Lord." I have been called into the fellowship of His Son. Paul has already told us in this epistle that all things are ours. He said that Paul and Apollos and Cephas and the world and life and death and things present and things to come are all ours, and we are Christ's. Life is ours, and I want to enjoy life. Death is ours, for we have the One who got the victory over death. Things present (the things of time) and things out yonder in the future are all ours. We are more than conquerors through Him who loved us!

CHAPTER 16

THEME: Final exhortations

In this chapter we will find a potpourri, that is, a collection of things. First Paul discusses the collection for the poor saints in Jerusalem, but then he goes on to discuss other things. He will talk about opportunities and opposition, about watching and praying, about the conduct of the church, about the acid test of doctrine, and about that which is ecclesiastical. The total church is in view here. Verses 1–4 concern the collection; verses 5–9 are personal—Paul discusses his personal plans; verses 10–24 deal with personalities, folk who walked down the streets of corrupt Corinth and lived for Christ.

THE COLLECTION

Now concerning the collection for the saints, as I have given order to the churches of Galatia, even so do ye [1 Cor. 16:1].

Paul begins this chapter by talking about taking up an offering! You would think that after Paul had discussed the Resurrection, that most glorious doctrine of the Christian faith, he would say, "Brethren, we are up in the heavenlies, so let's just stay up in the clouds." Instead, all of a sudden it seems like he has pulled out the plug. We find that we have just gone down to the very bottom. He is talking about a collection of money for the poor saints in Jerusalem.

Some pious folk say, "You shouldn't talk about a collection—that is a material matter. You should talk only of spiritual things." Generally those people don't want it talked about because the subject is a little bit embarrassing for them. Paul is going to lay out a method for Christian giving.

Now I hope you have your Bible open and that you will watch very carefully because I am not going to read it correctly. "On the Sabbath day let every one of you give tithes and offerings so that there will not be an offering when I come. It may be that when I get there we will have a special offering or probably a retiring offering." Somebody will say, "You surely didn't read it like it is." No, I didn't. But I read it the way it is often practiced today.

Now let us read it the way Paul wrote it.

> **Upon the first day of the week let every one of you lay by him in store, as God hath prospered him, that there be no gatherings when I come [1 Cor. 16:2].**

"Upon the first day of the week." If you don't meet on the first day of the week to worship God, then you will want to meet on that day to make your offering, which is a part of worship. That is ridiculous, of course. When he says to bring your offering on the first day of the week, this was the day on which the church came together to remember the Lord Jesus in His death and His resurrection. He rose on the first day of the week, which is Sunday, not the Sabbath day.

"Let every one of you lay by him in store, as God hath prospered him." He says nothing about tithes and offerings. They were to put aside their offerings as God had prospered them.

When I was pastoring a church in Texas, one of my officers owned several Coca-Cola plants, and one of them was in our town. He was a man of means, and he owned a ranch where we used to go to hunt and fish. Often he would ask me why I didn't preach on tithing. One day I said, "Why should I preach on tithing?" He said, "Because it is the Bible way of giving." I agreed, "Yes, it was the Old Testament way of giving, but under grace I don't believe tithing is the way it should be done." So he asked me, "How do you think it ought to be done?" I took him to this verse: "As God hath prospered him." Now this was during the depression. If you are as old as I am, you will remember that the depression in the 1930s was a very serious time. So I said to him, "For some strange reason, Coca-Cola is selling, and you are doing very well. However, there are some members in our church who couldn't give a tithe right now. I don't believe God is asking them to give a tenth. There are a few people who are doing well, and they are to give as they have been prospered—and they are not to stop with a tenth. Probably they ought to give a half." Do you know that this man never again suggested that I preach on tithing! The reason was that he was tithing, but he didn't want to give as God had prospered him.

"That there be no gatherings when I come." Paul didn't want his meeting with them to be spoiled by high pressure methods of taking up an offering. In my day I sometimes had to give as much attention to the offering as to dealing with new converts. Paul tells us how an offering should be collected.

> And when I come, whomsoever ye shall approve by your letters, them will I send to bring your liberality unto Jerusalem.
>
> And if it be meet that I go also, they shall go with me [1 Cor. 16:3–4].

Paul asks them to pick a committee to take the collection to Jerusalem with him. It is well for more than one man to be responsible for the offering. It is dangerous to turn the offering over to a single individual and let one man handle it. Is it that there is a doubt about a man's honesty if he is a Christian? Well, there may be. Even if a man is honest, there is a certain temptation involved. Paul gives us the best way to handle a collection. He uses very businesslike methods.

Paul talks here of their "liberality." It is interesting to study the words used for Christian giving. In our passage here he calls it a *logia* or "a collection." Then he speaks of their *charis* or "liberality"—that is the word for "grace." In Romans 15:26 a "contribution" is called a *koinōnia*, a fellowship. In 2 Corinthians 9:5 it is called a *eulogia*, which means "a bounty" or "a blessing." Second Corinthians 9:12 calls it a *diakonia*, which is "an administration" or "ministry." Acts 24:17 speaks of *alms—eleēmosunē*, which is "a kind act." All of these words refer to giving to the Lord, and each of these words can be used.

The interesting word here is "liberality," which should be *grace* giving. How has God blessed you? Could your giving to the Lord be considered liberality? In the Book of Leviticus instructions are given about tithing by God's people in the Old Testament. In the beginning the nation of Israel was a theocracy, and the tithes that the Israelites were to give supported both the government and the temple. They added up to about 30 percent of their total income. This gives us an indication of what the Israelite gave in the Old Testament under the economy of the Law. What do you think would be liberality under grace?

PERSONAL COMMENTS

Now I will come unto you, when I shall pass through Macedonia: for I do pass through Macedonia.

And it may be that I will abide, yea, and winter with you, that ye may bring me on my journey whithersoever I go [1 Cor. 16:5–6].

"Whithersoever I go" means that Paul doesn't know where he is going. Do you mean to tell me that the great Apostle of the Gentiles didn't have a blueprint or a road map from the Lord telling him everywhere he was to go? No, he says that the Lord just leads him along. Paul is in the wonderful position of being gloriously unsettled. He is not sure what he is to do. This is a great satisfaction to me because I don't know about the future either. There are folk in Christian service who tell me where they are going and what they will be doing five years from now. This worries me because I have never received directions like that from the Lord, and I hate to think they have a private line to the Lord that I don't have! Then when I read about Paul's not knowing what was ahead for him, it is a great comfort. To Paul and me the Lord doesn't give a road map; He just leads us from day to day. We are gloriously unsettled.

For I will not see you now by the way; but I trust to tarry a while with you, if the Lord permit [1 Cor. 16:7].

Paul is saying here that he does plan to go to Corinth, but only if the Lord permits it. Shouldn't we have plans? By all means we should make plans, but those plans always should be amenable to the will of God. We should be willing to change them. We should be willing to shuffle things around. When Paul went out, he did not have a rigid schedule for his missionary journeys. He went as the Lord led him. We see in the Book of Acts how the Lord just practically detoured him on the second missionary journey. Paul was going down into Asia; the Spirit of God sent him over to Europe. He didn't know he was going to Europe—he didn't have a visa for Europe—but in that day he didn't need a visa. He went where the Holy Spirit led him.

But I will tarry at Ephesus until Pentecost [1 Cor. 16:8].

That was his plan.

For a great door and effectual is opened unto me, and there are many adversaries [1 Cor. 16:9].

This is a wonderful verse that I have put with Revelation 3:8, (which is Christ's message to the church in Philadelphia): ". . . behold, I have set before thee an open door. . . ." And Paul says, "A great door and effectual is opened unto me." These two verses I have found to be true in the ministry God has given to me. Also it is true today that there are many adversaries. Any man who will stand for the Word of God has many enemies. That was the experience of Paul, and it has been my experience also. However, the Lord opens the door and no man can shut it. Thank God for that!

So we see Paul, gloriously happy, rejoicing in the will of God. If the lord wants him to go to Corinth, he will go.

PERSONALITIES

Now we come to the personalities. These were the folk who walked down the streets of Corinth. Corinth was a most corrupt city, a sensual city given over to immorality. They knew more about illicit sex than this generation knows today. Yet here were folk, walking the streets of Corinth, who knew the Lord Jesus and who lived for Him. They kept themselves unspotted from the world.

> Now if Timotheus come, see that he may be with you
> without fear: for he worketh the work of the Lord, as I
> also do.

> Let no man therefore despise him: but conduct him forth
> in peace, that he may come unto me: for I look for him
> with the brethren [1 Cor. 16:10–11].

Why would they despise Timothy? Paul wrote in 1 Timothy 4:12, "Let
no man despise thy youth. . . ." So he is telling the church in Corinth
to accept Timothy although he is a young man. He is a preacher of the
Word of God.

> As touching our brother Apollos, I greatly desired him
> to come unto you with the brethren: but his will was not
> at all to come at this time; but he will come when he
> shall have convenient time [1 Cor. 16:12].

Remember that the Corinthian church had divisions over Paul and
Apollos and Peter. But Paul loved Apollos, and he makes it clear that
they are serving the Lord together. He assures them that Apollos will
come to visit them at a later time.

> Watch ye, stand fast in the faith, quit you like men, be
> strong.

> Let all your things be done with charity [1 Cor.
> 16:13–14].

What words these are for us today!

> I beseech you, brethren, (ye know the house of
> Stephanas, that it is the firstfruits of Achaia, and that
> they have addicted themselves to the ministry of the
> saints,)

> That ye submit yourselves unto such, and to every one
> that helpeth with us, and laboureth [1 Cor. 16:15–16].

When we read that word *addicted,* we immediately think of drug addiction. But these people were addicted to the ministry of the saints. That was a great ministry!

He urges the Corinthians to submit to those who come to serve them.

I am glad of the coming of Stephanas and Fortunatus and Achaicus: for that which was lacking on your part they have supplied [1 Cor. 16:17].

They apparently made up the delegation that brought the letter from the Corinthian church over to Paul. Paul tells the folk in Corinth that these three Christian fellows were so wonderful that they made up for the whole church.

For they have refreshed my spirit and yours: therefore acknowledge ye them that are such [1 Cor. 16:18].

Paul is saying, "Give them a vote of thanks when they get back."

The churches of Asia salute you. Aquila and Priscilla salute you much in the Lord, with the church that is in their house [1 Cor. 16:19].

That is where many of these people came to know about Christ.

All the brethren greet you. Greet ye one another with an holy kiss [1 Cor. 16:20].

Is this a permit for kissing? It certainly is—if it is a holy kiss. Most kisses are not!

The salutation of me Paul with mine own hand [1 Cor. 16:21].

Paul dictated this epistle and then signed it.

If any man love not the Lord Jesus Christ, let him be Anathema Maranatha [1 Cor. 16:22].

The Lord Jesus asked Simon Peter, "Do you love Me? (see John 21:17). He didn't ask Peter if he would deny Him again. He just asked "Do you love Me?" That is the acid test today. Do you love Him?

Anathema means "accursed." Paul is saying, "If any one does not love the Lord, let him be accursed." Maranatha means "our Lord cometh."

The grace of our Lord Jesus Christ be with you.

My love be with you all in Christ Jesus. Amen [1 Cor. 16:23–24].

If you love the Lord Jesus, you will love the saints. The epistle closes on the high note of love.

BIBLIOGRAPHY
(Recommended for Further Study)

Boyer, James L. *For a World Like Ours: Studies in I Corinthians*. Grand Rapids, Michigan: Baker Book House, 1971. (Excellent for individual or group study.)

DeHaan, M. R. *Studies in First Corinthians*. Grand Rapids, Michigan: Zondervan Publishing House, 1956.

Gromacki, Robert G. *Called to Be Saints* (I Corinthians). Grand Rapids, Michigan: Baker Book House, n.d.

Gromacki, Robert G. *Stand Firm in the Faith* (II Corinthians). Grand Rapids, Michigan: Baker Book House, 1978.

Hodge, Charles. *An Exposition of First and Second Corinthians*. Carlisle, Pennsylvania: The Banner of Truth Trust, 1869. (For advanced students.)

Hughes, Philip E. *Paul's Second Epistle to the Corinthians*. Grand Rapids, Michigan: Wm. B. Eerdmans Publishing Co., 1962. (A comprehensive study.)

Ironside. H. A. *Addresses on First Corinthians*. Neptune, New Jersey: Loizeaux Brothers, 1938. (A fine survey.)

Kelly, William. *Notes on the First Epistle to the Corinthians*. Addison, Illinois: Bible Truth Publishers, 1878.

Kelly, William. *Notes on the Second Epistle to the Corinthians*. Addison, Illinois: Bible Truth Publishers, 1882.

Kent, Homer A., Jr. *A Heart Opened Wide: Studies in II Corinthians*. Grand Rapids, Michigan: Baker Book House, 1982. (Excellent.)

Luck, G. Coleman. *First Corinthians*. Chicago, Illinois: Moody Press, 1958. (A good survey.)

Luck, G. Coleman. *Second Corinthians*. Chicago, Illinois: Moody Press, 1960. (A good survey.)

Morgan, G. Campbell. *The Corinthian Letters of Paul*. Westwood, New Jersey: Fleming H. Revell Co., 1946.

Morris, Leon. *The First Epistle to the Corinthians*. Grand Rapids, Michigan: Wm. B. Eerdmans Publishing Co., 1958.

Moule, Handley C. G. *The Epistle of Second Corinthians*. Fort Washington, Pennsylvania: Christian Literature Crusade, n.d.

Robertson, A. T. *The Glory of the Ministry*. Grand Rapids, Michigan: Baker Book House, 1911. (Deals with II Corinthians 2:12—6:10, and should be read by every Christian worker.)

Tasker, R. V. G. *The Second Epistle of Paul to the Corinthians*. Grand Rapids, Michigan: Wm. B. Eerdmans Publishing Co., 1958.

Vine, W. E. *First Corinthians*. Grand Rapids, Michigan: Zondervan Publishing House, 1951.